W9-CSB-763

WITHDRAWN

Tyler Florence

CELEBRITY CHEFS

Tyler Florence

Sherri Mabry Gordon

Enslow Publishing

101 W. 23rd Street
Suite 240
New York, NY 10011
USA

enslow.com

Published in 2017 by Enslow Publishing, LLC
101 W. 23rd Street, Suite 240, New York, NY 10011

Copyright © 2017 by Enslow Publishing, LLC.
All rights reserved.

No part of this book may be reproduced by any means without the written permission of the publisher.

Library of Congress Cataloging-in-Publication Data
Names: Gordon, Sherri Mabry, author.
Title: Tyler Florence / Sherri Mabry Gordon.
Other titles: Celebrity chefs.
Description: New York, NY : Enslow Publishing, 2017. | "2017 | Series: Celebrity chefs | Includes bibliographical references and index.
Identifiers: LCCN 2016005254 | ISBN 9780766077560 (library bound)
Subjects: LCSH: Florence, Tyler—Juvenile literature. | Cooks—United States—Biography—Juvenile literature. | Celebrity chefs—United States—Biography—Juvenile literature.
Classification: LCC TX649.F554 G67 2017 | DDC 641.5092—dc23
LC record available at http://lccn.loc.gov/2016005254

Printed in the United States of America

To Our Readers: We have done our best to make sure all website addresses in this book were active and appropriate when we went to press. However, the author and the publisher have no control over and assume no liability for the material available on those websites or on any websites they may link to. Any comments or suggestions can be sent by e-mail to customerservice@enslow.com.

Photo Credits: Star icon throughout book: Yulia Glam/Shutterstock.com; cover, p. 3 Jemal Countess/WireImage/Getty Images; p. 6 Tom Briglia/FilmMagic/Getty Images; p. 9 Jerry Cleveland/The Denver Post via Getty Images; p. 11 ZUMA Press, Inc./Alamy Stock Photo; p. 14 Anthony Heflin/Shutterstock.com; p. 18 Frazer Harrison/Getty Images; p. 21 Jamie-Andrea Yanak/AP Images; p. 23 Peter Power/Toronto Star via Getty Images; p. 25 Tampa Bay Times/Zuma Press; p. 27 Judie Burstein/Globe Photos/Zuma Press; pp. 30, 36 PRNewsFoto/Food Network/AP Images; p. 40 John Sciulli/Getty Images for DCP; p. 42 National Archives/File:Sanfranciscoearthquake1906.jpg/Wikimedia Commons; pp. 44, 54 Eric Risberg/AP Images; p. 48 SJ Weiss/Sara Jaye Weiss/Newscom; p. 58 Aaron Davidson/Getty Images for Food Network SoBe Wine & Food Festival; p. 63 Ben Gabbe/Getty Images; p. 67 Bon Appetit/Alamy Stock Photo; p. 68 Larry Busacca/Getty Images for NYCWFF; p. 70 Wellcome Library, London. Wellcome Images images@wellcome.ac.uk http://wellcomeimages.org A kitchen. Opera... Bartolomeo Scappi Published: 1570; p. 74 George Rose/Getty Images; p. 78 Trisha Leeper/Getty Images for Canon; p. 82 Ben Gabbe/Getty Images; p. 85 J. L. Sousa/Napa Valley Register/Zuma Press; p. 86 Bill Hogan/Chicago Tribune/MCT via Getty Images; p. 91 Neilson Barnard/Getty Images for NYCWFF; p. 97 Bobby Bank/WireImage/Getty Images; p. 99 David Livingston/Getty Images; p. 100 Iryna Melnyk/Shutterstock.com; p. 101 Brent Hofacker/Shutterstock.com; p. 103 Crazychristina/iStock/Thinkstock; p. 105 AmalliaEka/iStock/Thinkstock; p. 107 Elena Demyanko/Shutterstock.com; p. 109 svariophoto/Shutterstock.com; p. 112, 116, 122 Brent Hofacker/Shutterstock.com; p. 114 MSPhotographic/Shutterstock.com; p. 119 buengza/Shutterstock.com.

CONTENTS

1   The Beginnings of a Chef   7

2   The Making of a Star   20

3   Tyler and His Restaurants   38

4   Tyler's Cookbooks   57

5   What It Means to Be a Celebrity Chef   73

6   Tyler's Causes   89

7   Try It Yourself!   100

Selected Resources by Tyler Florence   125

Chronology   126

Chapter Notes   127

Glossary   138

Further Reading   140

Index   142

Tyler Florence is more than a chef. He is also a businessman, a restauranteur, and a television host.

The Beginnings of
a Chef

Born in Greenville, South Carolina, on March 3, 1971, Kevin Tyler Florence didn't always want to be a chef. In fact, it wasn't a desire to cook that first drove him into a kitchen at all. At fifteen years old, his desire for a car introduced him into the world of restaurants. "When I was fifteen, I really wanted a car. My parents told me I would have to get a job and save my money if I wanted something."[1]

At the time, his girlfriend's parents owned the nicest restaurant in Greenville, South Carolina, so it seemed logical that he would get a job there. Little did Tyler know, that decision would set him on a path to success as a chef.

Tyler started out as a dishwasher. But it wasn't long before he fell in love with the energy of the kitchen, he says. "I moved from the dish station to prep and then working on the line fairly quickly. It was the first thing I was ever really good at. At that moment, I knew I wanted to be a chef for the rest of my life."[2]

It certainly helped that the French chef Tyler was learning from was somewhat of a celebrity in the small town. "[That] chef was a god to me. He drove a Harley, and women stopped by to see him every night. I thought, that's what I want to do," Tyler explains.[3] "I've since learned that cooks are like misfit poets—they travel the globe to learn from world-class chefs. They're socially unacceptable, and they work with their hands. I fell in love with the whole thing."[4]

Learning from the Best

While working as a line cook in South Carolina, Tyler says he used his meager earnings to take the train to New York City one night. "I spent an entire paycheck on dinner at Jean-Georges Vongerichten's restaurant, JoJo. That was a tipping moment [for me]—I came home with empty pockets, a matchbook, and ideas."[5]

Tyler says he further broadened his culinary perspective with a trip to Paris at age nineteen. "I was totally broke. I ate only tomatoes, cheese, and baguettes, but it opened my eyes. Whenever I speak to culinary students, I tell them, 'Max out your credit cards, take your knife kit and your Michelin Guide, go knock on a chef's door, and tell him you want to cook. Do it for free if you have to. The experience will change your life.'"[6]

Following his life-changing trip to Paris, Tyler further broadened his culinary perspective by attending the prestigious culinary program at Johnson and Wales University in Charleston, South Carolina. There he learned some valuable lessons that he still carries with him to this day.

For instance, Tyler says in his first year of culinary school at Johnson and Wales that "Chef Victor Sumuro walked over to my station, picked up my knife and felt the sharpness of the blade with his thumb. He laid it down, made eye contact with me and

Johnson and Wales University was started as a business school by Gertrude I. Johnson and Mary T. Wales. The College of Culinary Arts is the largest food service education program in the world, as well as one of the most reknowned.

said, 'Dull knife, dull chef.' I never forgot that, and my knives have been razor blades ever since."[7]

After graduating from the program, Tyler decided to take on the Big Apple. "A week after I graduated, I packed my meager belongings and moved to Brooklyn," he says.[8]

There he took the helm of some of the most acclaimed restaurants in the city. It wasn't long before he established himself as one of New York City's finest young stars. While in New York, he perfected his culinary skills under the guidance of the some of the city's top chefs, including Charlie Palmer of Aureole.

Today, Palmer is a master chef and hospitality entrepreneur who has received critical acclaim. He is best known for his Progressive American cuisine, which is built on lively flavors and unexpected combinations. He also infuses everything with a classical French technique.[9] Even today, you can see a hint of Palmer's cooking style in Tyler's food. Yet, it is clear Tyler has taken what he has learned from the best and made it uniquely his own.

Tyler also worked under Marta Pulini at Mad 61 and Rick Laakkonen. Chef Pulini has since brought her cuisine all around the world, from New York to the Olympic Games of London. She is now pursuing her food and wine concept in Milan.[10] Meanwhile, Rick Laakkonen is the executive chef at Jake's Steakhouse in East Meadow, New York.

Branching Out on His Own

Confident of his culinary talent, Tyler accepted the executive chef's position at Cibo in 1995, where his original creations received applause from numerous New York City publications, such as the *New York Times*, *New York Magazine,* and *Crain's New York Business.*

In 1998, Tyler ventured out on his own, opening the critically acclaimed Cafeteria in Manhattan's trendy Chelsea neighborhood. Under his direction, the restaurant received a nomination for "Best New Restaurant" in *Time Out* New York.[11]

Overall, the restaurant was a huge success, which led to various guest appearances on the Food Network. Eventually, Florence was signed to host the cable network's *Food 911*. The handsome chef went on to host *How to Boil Water, Tyler's Ultimate, The Great Food Truck Race,* and various other Food

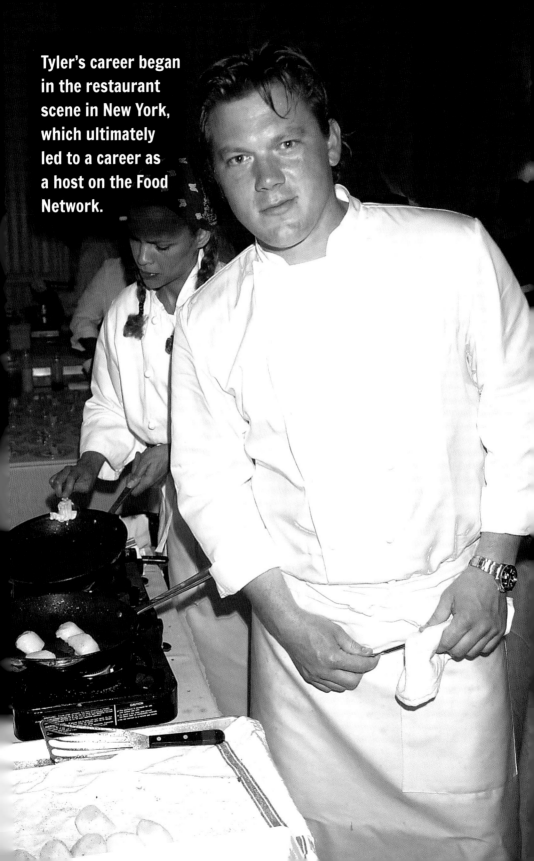

Tyler's career began in the restaurant scene in New York, which ultimately led to a career as a host on the Food Network.

Network specials. Since then, Tyler has delighted the masses by sharing the sights, sounds, and flavors of his unique culinary vision with fans around the world.

As a result, Tyler's popularity skyrocketed. And in 2003, *People* magazine named Tyler the "sexiest chef alive." The following year, at the Sundance Film Festival, Tyler met Tolan Clark, his (now) wife. At the time, Tolan worked in public relations for chefs Wolfgang Puck and Rocco DiSpirito.[12]

It was actually celebrity chef Rocco DiSpirito who introduced them. And they are the perfect match. Both Tyler and Tolan are genuine, down-to-earth people committed to their family and business ventures. In fact, according to J. M. Hirsch of the *Huffington Post*, Tolan, like Tyler, is so sincere and pleasant that it is "hard to believe she arose from a world saturated by celebrity." According to Hirsch: her parents were introduced by filmmaker and director Francis Ford Coppola, and she had at one time worked for Ryan Seacrest.[13]

Today, the couple lives in California, Tolan's home state. They moved there when she became pregnant with their first child. They now have two children together, and a third, a son, Miles, that Tyler had with first wife, Christie Leer.

> *"You are a product of your path. What you do, who you work for, and how you carry yourself along that path adds up to who you are as a professional. Keep your path in top shape."*

A Style All His Own

Despite the multitude of cooking styles to which Tyler has been exposed, he has cultivated a style that is uniquely his own. "I've eaten my way around the world and I am a die-hard fan of many different cooking styles. But my cooking style—the style of food that keeps me up at night trying to decode my own ideas—is gorgeous American cooking. Pure and simple."[14]

In the early years of Tyler's career, he says his American cooking philosophy was actually a hindrance. "If I said 'American,' off the bat people assumed burgers and fries. If you didn't stand behind the Italian flag, the Japanese flag, or the Spanish flag, no one took you seriously."[15]

Today, Tyler's recipes and approaches to food, which are often perfected in his test kitchen, have people clamoring for reservations in his restaurants and buying his cookbooks as soon as they hit the shelves. He even has imparted his style into his other ventures, including a line of healthy baby food.

Still Down to Earth

Yet all of this prestige and success has not changed Tyler. In fact, according to Susan Dyer Reynolds, a writer for *Northside San Francisco*, "of all the celebrity chefs I've met, Tyler Florence takes the cake for the most down to earth and genuine. He has worked hard for his success, and after just a few moments of conversation, it becomes obvious that he never takes a moment of it for granted."[16]

And it shows in the advice Tyler frequently passes on to young chefs studying under him. He tells them: "Don't let your ego get in the way. As a chef, you have to provide the best customer service, period. You have to be willing to take your product and filter it, take your business model and filter it and let a lot of people give you feedback and break it down before you go live."[17]

Lover of the Outdoors

Despite his big-city experiences, Tyler still enjoys being outdoors: "I grew up on a cul-de-sac in a subdivision in upstate South Carolina. Behind it was an undeveloped area of the Blue Ridge Mountains that we used to run and play in.

Tyler grew up in the Blue Ridge Mountains in South Carolina. Because of this, he still enjoys spending time outdoors.

Fast Facts
★ **about Tyler**

His go-to entertaining dish: His famous fried chicken.

His favorite food gifts: Small jars of honey. Tyler and Tolan have three thousand Italian honeybees in their backyard that produce "a clear, golden honey that smells like the air around Mount Tam, with wildflowers and wild fennel," Tyler says. "We package it in small six-ounce jars that we label with the name of the recipient. Hopefully, it will take them a few months to work their way through the jar, so any morning they pop a piece of toast into the toaster and spread on some honey, they can remember it's something we made for them."[18]

His gift to his managers and chefs: Personalized Moleskine notebooks with their names embossed on them. "As a chef I don't leave the house unless I have my Moleskine, because when an idea hits you, you can either record it there on the spot or it drifts off to the land of nevermore," Tyler says. "Writing in a Moleskine also feels more organic than tapping in notes into a computer. You can also judge the idea by your handwriting—if it's fluid and full of creativity, or stressed and tight."[19]

His entertaining tip: Be calm and relaxed when your guests arrive and plan a menu that is not too large or too aggressive. He says that if you do take on too much, nobody leaves with anything fantastic. "It is much better to make something clean and simple and delicious and let that be it," he says.[20]

His favorite family spot: Stinson Beach, a sleepy little town about forty-five minutes north of the Golden Gate Bridge in San Francisco, California. "It's a six-mile-long beach, populated by no more than about one thousand people year-round," Tyler says. "We spent a week there and it was magic. Because we have small

15

kids, we are into instant gratification when it comes to vacations, because hopping on a plane with them is a bit of a challenge."[21]

His most-requested recipe: Fried chicken. "It's not Southern fried, it's California fried," Tyler says. "It has turned out to be this defining dish in [my Wayfare] Restaurant and I'm very proud of it."[22]

The dish he recommends everyone knows how to make: Bolognese sauce. "It's always a hit," he says.[23]

His favorite city: Miami. "I travel all the time. I was on the road 280 days last year doing different shows for the Food Network. You can talk to people, read books, and taste food, but you never really get to know a place until you actually go there," he says. "Miami is beautiful, it's warm, and the people are friendly. In some places, like Boston or Washington, DC, there's a really heavy energy, and in others you just know you are in the right spot. That's what Miami is for me. I get off the plane and the stress just leaves my shoulders."[24]

The hardest technique to learn: Braising. "I think braising can be complicated," he says. "To me, one of the most important techniques I've needed to master is a deep-tasting meat braise, and that's starting with the basics. Any good chef will tell you, 'The more I know; the more I don't know.' That's why there's an endless fascination of learning new techniques. You never know it all or learn everything."[25]

His expectation when it comes to food: Simple: he doesn't like bad food. "People ask me if I'm picky, but I just want to appreciate what the expectation is," Tyler explains. "A diner is different from Dean Fearing's in Dallas. My expectation is different, but I'm excited for both."[26]

"When people don't know what they're doing in the kitchen, that reflects the situation," he adds. "There's literally nothing that I don't like or a flavor profile that doesn't work. I can make anchovies and peanut butter taste great."[27]

In summer, we'd leave in the morning and not come home until the sun went down. My parents didn't know where I was. There was this sense of responsibility where you just got lost outside, and your day was your own. But you knew how to get home—you had this homing pigeon sort of thing that a lot of kids don't possess today."[28]

This is just the kind of experience he wants to share with his own children, he says. "I'm carving a semi–Tough Mudder trail on our property, which is wooded and hasn't been touched in one hundred years. I have a machete I got on Amazon. I don't know what kind it is, but it's a bushwhacker. I'm cutting the briar patches so that we can turn them into something else. I'm also bending young eucalyptus trees into tunnels. I have a long-term vision, but it'll probably change. I've kind of turned mountain goat."[29]

Overall, Tyler says he doesn't believe in restricting his children from technology. "But I do believe in balancing it out," he says. "So we hike a lot. I lived [more than a decade] in New York City, but now we live on six acres in Corte Madera, California—my wife and I moved west in 2006, when she was pregnant with our son."[30]

Carving Out His Own Path

Tyler has come a long way in a short period of time. Aside from being an easily recognizable face on the Food Network and the esteemed chef of several restaurants, he also is the best-selling author of a number of cookbooks, as well as a children's book titled *Tyler Makes Pancakes*. He also has several other business ventures and is passionate about feeding the hungry in the United States. As a result, it is not surprising that Tyler's laid-back style has millions around the country raving about his

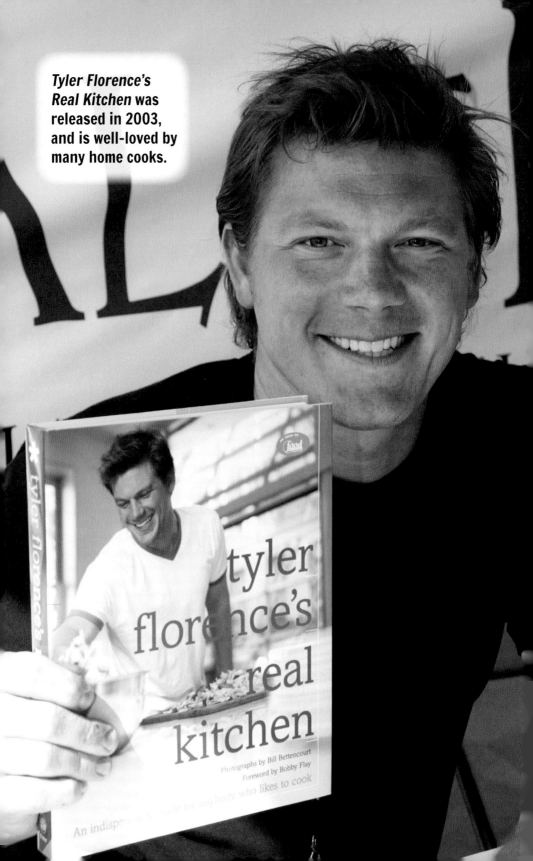

Tyler Florence's Real Kitchen was released in 2003, and is well-loved by many home cooks.

cookbooks, visiting his restaurants, and watching his television programs.

"The most important advice I give my cooks is that you are a product of your path," Tyler says. "What you do, who you work for, and how you carry yourself along that path adds up to who you are as a professional. Keep your path in top shape." And that is exactly what Tyler has done. There isn't a chef out there with a clearer path ahead of him than Tyler Florence.[31]

Chapter

2

The Making of
a Star

Tyler is one of the original stars of the Food Network, gracing American television screens for more than sixteen years. "His easy manner in the kitchen and baby-face good looks wooed viewers early and kept him afloat even as his field got crowded," says J. M. Hirsch of the *Huffington Post*.[1]

In the early years of his career, Tyler caught the eye of Food Network executives while he was the executive chef of Cafeteria in New York City. As word of Tyler's charismatic personality and exceptional food spread, Food Network executives had to see what all the fuss was about.

They recognized his star quality and quickly brought him into the folds of the company. He starred in such series as *How to Boil Water*, *Food 911*, and his signature show, *Tyler's Ultimate*. He also has hosted numerous other Food Network shows and is a regular guest on *The Today Show*, *CNN*, *The View*, *The Tonight Show*, *Oprah*, *Access Hollywood*, *Extra*, and *Good Morning America*.

Because Tyler was formally trained as a chef, it was easy for viewers to follow his instructions. His down-to-earth nature and simple recipes made him a hit with Food Network viewers.

"Being on television wasn't what my path was," Tyler says. "It just happened to fall in my lap and I embraced it because I figured if I didn't I wouldn't know what it was like."[2]

What's more, Tyler is humble about his celebrity status and works hard to maintain credibility as a trained chef. "I understand what [the viewers'] preconceived notions [might be]. [They] watch the Food Network and there's a lot of people on there [with] a range of cooking abilities in terms of what they can do and what they can't do . . . Someone who watches Food Network might say: 'These aren't established chefs so much as they are home cooks with a good smile and some zippy one liners.' . . . But you walk into [any of my restaurants] and you see we are as serious as any other restaurant in America."[3]

> *"I think it's important for everyone to feel failure. I wouldn't trade any stupid decision for another five years of life."*

Cutting His Teeth at Food Network

With two early shows including *How to Boil Water* and *Food 911,* Tyler gained experience at the Food Network before being offered his signature show, *Tyler's Ultimate.* In the beginning, he admits that it was tough to move from restaurants to television.

"It was a learning curve," he says. "There was a lot of experimentation. Television production, a lot like a day in a restaurant, can take twelve plus hours to shoot. I had a lot of stamina and was willing to do just about anything for the shot."[4]

Tyler's easy manner struck a chord with viewers who were intimidated by cooking. He helped many fans conquer their fears of the kitchen.

He also says his recipe writing for the show wasn't as polished as it is now. "I was cooking food that was too complicated to produce at home," he says. "After a few seasons, I finally got it. Less was more. Recipes that had fewer, better ingredients and a simple but solid technique played out on television the way they were supposed to—friendly and approachable."[5]

But, he says that after he found his voice on television, his television career skyrocketed. The key was using a voice that was different from his restaurant voice. Finding a voice that was easy to understand, cordial, and one that simplified instructions was key.

How to Boil Water

This was one of the first shows on the Food Network and began broadcasting in 1993. Originally hosted by Emeril Lagasse, the show was promoted by the Food Network as a personal cooking school for viewers and focused on simple cooking for those who have little to no cooking skills.

As Emeril's popularity grew, he eventually moved on to his own show, *Essence of Emeril*. Several hosts later, Tyler took the helm along with cooking-challenged cohost, Jack Hourigan. The goal was to educate the audience on "making quick and easy main courses, scrumptious sides, decadent desserts, and even complete menus perfect for company."[6]

Food 911

This show was designed for anyone suffering from food dilemmas. During the early seasons of this show, which began in 1999 on the Food Network, Tyler went into family kitchens across the United States and made something awesome with whatever he could find in their pantry and refrigerator. Later,

As Tyler's popularity grew, fans looked to him for advice on food, cooking, and how to stock their kitchens.

the show involved less travel. Instead, Tyler showed viewers how to fix everything from fallen soufflés to overcooked chicken.

Tyler's Ultimate

Tyler began producing *Tyler's Ultimate* while still shooting episodes of his original show, *Food 911*. The premise of this show was to make "ultimate" versions of popular or common dishes. And the show allowed Tyler to showcase his creativity and his passion for trying new things.

When the show first aired, the Food Network was actively creating traveling food shows, and in *Tyler's Ultimate*, Tyler traveled and cooked on the program. For instance, he would travel around the world to discover different versions of a particular dish. The goal was to discover the ultimate version of the dish. Then, at the end of the episode, Tyler would combine his notes and the recipes he had learned from traveling and add his own spin. In the end, he created the "ultimate" recipe of the dish.

Eventually, the show's format changed and the traveling was removed. As a result, the show morphed into Tyler sharing his "ultimate" versions of various recipes. There was a lot more teaching and cooking on later versions of the show.

The Race Continues for Tyler at Food Network

One of the more popular shows that Tyler hosts on the Food Network is *The Great Food Truck Race*. During the program, seven real teams representing the best food trucks in the United States hit the road to cook their way across America.

Tyler's Ultimate combined elements of several recipes that Tyler researched for each dish.

The Pinnacle of Stardom:
Cooking for the President

During President Barack Obama's reelection campaign, Tyler got the rare opportunity to cook for the president and several other celebrities. The event took place in Tampa, Florida, in the backyard of Lisa DeBartolo (daughter of former San Francisco 49ers owner Eddie DeBartolo Jr.). According to the Obama Foodorama report, the fund-raising event cost $20,000 per plate. Even Eddie Vedder was there, a singer and songwriter best known as a member of the rock band Pearl Jam.

To dazzle the guests and give them their money's worth, Tyler served burrata (a fresh, unstretched mozzarella) mixed with basil, peach, and berries. He also served squash and quail egg ravioli. Another dish was chicken-fried quail with key limes and herbs; garnished with crispy pork belly and a banana mustard. It was completed with corn pudding, zucchini confit, and smoked almond foam. Meanwhile, his Wayfare Tavern pastry chef, Matt Masera, prepared coconut shortbread, with key lime–parsley curd, blackberry, and vanilla-lime pavlova.

Tyler's wife, Tolan, documented the event via Twitter. She tweeted: "Secret service let us in with our cell phones. Going to tweet from dinner with @BarackObama."[7]

Each week, the teams that sell the most food move on to the next episode, while the losing team has to turn in the keys to their truck. At the end of the show, only one food truck remains and drives away with a $50,000 grand prize.

The rules are simple. In each city, the teams start with a limited budget, and then they have the weekend to strategize and sell. Anything they buy beyond their budget comes out of their profits. Whichever team makes the most money is safe. The truck that makes the least amount of money is eliminated.[8]

Aside from being one of the most entertaining shows on Food Network, it also has impacted the food truck industry. In fact, Tyler notes that prior to the beginning of the show, the food truck business was completely different; and points out the significance the show has had on the industry. For instance, more and more culinary-inclined trucks are popping up around the country. There are even food truck festivals and events. "Street meat" is common throughout North America. Many young chefs today, rather than open a restaurant, begin their careers with food trucks. Food trucks are cheaper, simpler to run, and easier to bring to the masses.

"What I love about [the show] is we've disrupted the entire restaurant industry," Tyler says. "Like, I own restaurants in San Francisco, and if I had to kind of redo my life, if I were twenty-five, I think food trucks are a fantastic business model. Just the return on investment is insane."[9]

"So instead of raising $2 [million], $3 [million] or $4 million for a restaurant, people are putting $25,000 or $30,000 into a business. And they can be in business the next weekend," Tyler explains. "You lease a truck, you skin it, you'll go get a food handler's permit, then go to Costco and buy a bunch of stuff, and then you're really on the road. And you can serve the

As host of *The Great Food Truck Race*, Tyler didn't do much cooking, but he did learn about a new way to be a chef and to own a restaurant.

same amount of units out of a food truck as you could [in a] restaurant."[10]

What's more, the show has attracted some very high-quality food trucks. And they are traveling some impressive routes on the show. For instance in one episode, the trucks went from Santa Monica to Chicago on the famous Route 66.

"It was amazing just to check out that historical route through America's heartland," Tyler says. "And you can sort of just watch the transition going from LA to the desert, and then we're in the desert for a long time and Texas, and then up to the Midwest. It [was] a first for the show."[11]

There also were some surprises along the way, Tyler says. "We've never had more emergencies throughout the season, like, situations got very real very quickly. Taking food trucks on a three thousand-mile road trip has its ups and downs for sure, and our competitors [fight] like they wanted [this] for life."[12]

Tyler says food trucks are this generation's answers to American fast food. "We've done it. We've created a whole other business model that a lot of young people are getting into, and it's cool, it's fashionable, it's edgy."[13]

Overall, Tyler says he's proud to host *The Great Food Truck Race*. "[I like] looking back at what we've done to really change the American landscape. Six years ago, starting this conversation, doing television interviews and radio interviews, nobody got it—it sounded gross. And now there couldn't be a trend that's hotter in the food world than food trucks."[14]

Tyler's Advice for Food Truck Entrepreneurs

Tyler says he is honored when people reach out to him and ask for food truck advice. "When they do, the first thing I tell them is they have to specialize in something, and that they need to have their category."[15]

For example, he says everyone loves tacos, "but it needs a design, pop, and it needs to say what the truck does. People will give you about two seconds when they first see your truck to decide whether it looks good or not."[16]

"So the overall concept has to be simple," he says. "Also, the execution has to be phenomenal. You need to be obsessed with your product, and really have a passion for it."[17]

Tyler says food truck owners also have to have hospitality in their blood. "People who think this is just a business opportunity may fall out of love with it fairly fast just because you have to really enjoy putting a smile on somebody's face."[18]

He also suggests being objective and studying the market inside and out. "You need to be able to look at your truck and your product and form an objective opinion about whether your truck is going to be competitive or not. You have to analyze what you're selling and make comparisons in the marketplace, and if it's not the best in your category figure out what you're doing wrong and how to fix it."[19]

All in all, Tyler says successful food trucks have identified a concept, have a crystal-clear brand identity, conduct research, and develop [their] product. "[The] product needs to be of an exceptionally high quality—perfect, essentially—and [the owner has] to completely understand the marketplace before even thinking about opening a food truck."[20]

Other Food Network Shows

Tyler also hosts several other shows on the Food Network. These include *Worst Cooks in America*, *Food Court Wars*, and

Best Cook in America. These shows each offer something different for audiences.

Worst Cooks in America

On this show, Tyler and fellow Food Network star, Anne Burrell, each lead a team of recruits through seven weeks of culinary boot-camp-like experiences trying to help them learn from their cooking mistakes. And they do make mistakes— lots of them. In the end, only one recruit will remain and win $25,000. They also should be able to shed the title of Worst Cook in America.

Food Court Wars

On *Food Court Wars*, two teams of aspiring food entrepreneurs battle against one another to win their own food court restaurant, rent-free for a year. In each episode, there is a different US city mall that wants to open a brand-new local eatery in the food court. The goal is to fill the space with a fresh, region-specific menu, according to the Food Network.

Throughout the show, Tyler offers guidance to the teams on how to test their concept, market their brand, and run their outlet for a full day of feeding hungry shoppers. The team that makes the most money gets to keep their eatery space, which is worth more than $100,000.[21]

America's Best Cook

Hosted by Ted Allen, the Food Network brings home cooks into the most intense arena in America. The goal is to determine who can take home the honors as the best cook in America.

Four Food Network stars, including Cat Cora, Alex Guarnaschelli, Michael Symon, and Tyler Florence, represent

Common
★ Cooking Mistakes

Mistake # 1: Over mixing

According to the Food Network, you should always mix dough and batter carefully and gently, unless the recipe tells you to kneed vigorously. Instead, slowly fold in the ingredients—especially in batters for quick breads and muffins. Overmixing can lead to toughness.[22]

Mistake #2: Not Resting Meats and Casseroles

Even though everything looks and smells great, be sure you hold off a little bit before digging in. Meats and baked dishes like lasagna need to sit a few minutes after coming out of the oven. Doing so allows the juices to stay in the meat and the layers of a baked dish to hold together instead of sliding around.[23]

Mistake #3: Slicing Meat With the Grain

In steaks and roasts, there are long "strings" that run along the meat. This is called the grain and you want to slice against it. If you don't, your meat will be chewy and tough.[24]

Mistake #4: Using a Dull Knife

Although it sounds counterintuitive, you are more likely to cut yourself with a dull knife than you are with a sharp one. Dull knives slip more easily. What's more, your food will slice and dice effortlessly and consistently when you use a sharp knife.[25]

Mistake #5—Not Tasting Your Food

Tasting as you cook is probably one of the most important parts of cooking. After all, how will you know if you are serving something good if you do not taste it? Tasting and seasoning your food as you go should be a regular part of your cooking routine.[26]

four different regions of the country. As a result, they choose two home cooks to compete on their team and battle through an increasingly difficult set of challenges.

The coaches, including Tyler, dedicate themselves to developing their team and mentoring their cooks. If their cooks go home, then they are done. So the goal is that their team would stay in the competition and ultimately become the best cook in America.[27]

Take the Good with the Bad

While Tyler has experienced a great deal of success on the Food Network, there were times when things were challenging. In fact, at one point in Tyler's career there were not enough advertising dollars to fund his shows on the Food Network.

"The world fell apart," Tyler says. "We had just moved to California and the economy collapsed. My wife and I were just terrified. Food Network canceled two of my seasons because they literally didn't have the ad money to pay for it."[28]

In fact, according to J. M. Hirsch of the *Huffington Post*, Tyler built his empire almost entirely on celebrity. "It didn't occur to him that this might not be a good thing."[29]

"All of the public appearance business dried up overnight," Tyler says. "It's almost like the business model that was just sort of handed to me, and I took for granted, was gone. I was like, `Wow! I don't think this stream of water will ever run out.' And when it did, I was really terrified . . ."[30]

"We were naive enough to think all this glorious fun stuff could last forever," he adds, "and we weren't smart enough to really kind of establish a series of businesses that truly speak our language and give us a sense of stability. So we said, when we get out of this, we're not doing this the same way as before."[31]

Tyler teamed up with fellow celebrity chef Anne Burrell to teach *America's Worst Cooks*.

As a result, instead of following the dictates of a network or fame, Tyler followed his passions the second time around. So when the Food Network offered him a new series—*The Great Food Truck Race*—Tyler wasn't convinced it was right for him. But he agreed.

Then the show took off. And he fell in love, not just with the show, but with its concept—helping people with big dreams make them real. As a result, Tyler says he loves investing in other people's ideas.

Because Tyler has had it all and lost it all, he sees value in both. "I think it's important for everyone to feel failure. I wouldn't trade any stupid decision for another five years of life," Tyler says. "We have [several] restaurants, a retail store, baby food, a television division, a publishing division, and I've never been happier."[32]

Chapter

3

Tyler and
His Restaurants

Tyler prides himself on being an all-American cook who embraces simple flavors and fresh ingredients. And all of his restaurants radiate this philosophy. To date, Tyler has three California restaurants, which include Wayfare Tavern in San Francisco, El Paseo in Mill Valley, and Napa Farms Market (also known as Tyler Florence Fresh) in the San Francisco International Airport.

And his talent and hard work at each establishment shows. He was awarded "Restaurateur of the Year" and has consistently earned three-star reviews from San Francisco restaurant critics. He also has been nominated twice for a James Beard award in the category "Best Chef, West."

"All three of my restaurants . . . are my happy places," Tyler says. "It's where I can teach the guys in the kitchen how to love and respect the ingredients in front of them. It keeps my mind sharp [because] we are constantly experimenting with new techniques and better ways to get to the truth in food. When I see someone's eyes roll back in [his] head because the food is so good, that's the most fulfilling feeling I can have as a professional."[1]

East Coast to West Coast

Tyler got his first experience as a chef in New York City. Thus, many people found it surprising when he moved to California. The idea came about when his wife, Tolan, became pregnant with their first child. Their plan was to leave New York and head to Mill Valley, California, to be closer to her family.

Initially, their plan was that Tyler would tinker with making wine, open a retail store, and maybe start a restaurant. They were counting on his celebrity status, his shows on the Food Network, and his television appearances to support them. But when the economy fell flat, so did the need for a celebrity chef.

Consequently, Tyler and Tolan were forced to rethink their plans. And the most sensible conclusion was for Tyler to get back to his roots—the thing that led to his stardom in the first place—his abilities as a chef. As a result, he set forth with plans to open a restaurant in San Francisco. But the city's prominent food scene was skeptical.

"When Wayfare Tavern opened in 2010, the reception was lukewarm," writes J. M. Hirsch of the *Huffington Post*. "Who was this New Yorker who thought he could just march into the city's cutthroat restaurant scene?"[2]

San Francisco is a very competitive restaurant town, Tyler says. "To stay on top, you have to be a little better than you were yesterday."[3]

The people of San Francisco assumed that he had not done his homework and that he didn't know anything about the San Francisco clientele, Tyler recalls. "I remember one review where the writer complained that he couldn't get a reservation for

Tyler and fellow celebrity chef Masaharu Morimoto (right) have fun on the red carpet of the Los Angeles Food & Wine unveiling in 2011.

weeks and then eventually got his meal to go, ate it in the alley behind the restaurant and published a picture of his half-eaten chicken. It was a little crazy."[4]

Eventually though, the people of San Francisco accepted Wayfare Tavern as part of the landscape. But it took time. Tyler says in the meantime, he focused on letting the food and restaurant speak for itself and "before long people came around to the fact that we were doing something incredible."[5]

"Wayfare Tavern really is unlike any other San Francisco restaurant," Tyler explains. "We wanted to build a restaurant that [looks like it] survived the earthquake of 1906. Nothing in the financial district really did survive the quake. So we did a ton of research and replicated what a restaurant would have looked like back then. We thought the place needed to take you somewhere, needed to be transformative. That, and the food is out of this world."[6]

> "*When I see someone's eyes roll back in [his] head because the food is so good, that's the most fulfilling feeling I can have as a professional.*"

Wayfare Tavern

Wayfare Tavern, which opened in San Francisco's Financial District, is in the former Rubicon space, one of San Francisco's most celebrated restaurants. The restaurant owners had called it quits in 2008, and the space sat empty for more than a year,

The earthquake of 1906 shook the city of San Francisco so hard that whole sections of the city crumbled.

So when the opportunity presented itself, Tyler knew he had to seize it.

"Wayfare Tavern is without a question one of the most important opportunities I've ever had," Tyler says. "One of the building owners, who is now my business partner, met me at our gym one morning in 2009. [He] mentioned Rubicon to me, and I almost freaked out. I never had a chance to eat there when it was Rubicon, but I was very aware of the caliber of chefs that the restaurant graduated—chefs that would go on to put San Francisco on the culinary map."[7]

However, taking over the Rubicon building and establishing a new restaurant there would not be easy. Aside from the skeptical culinary scene in San Francisco, "it was 2009 and the economy was in the tank," Tyler says.[8]

But he did not let these facts deter him and started doing research on the building. "The neighborhood also had a fascinating story as the center of the red-light district known as the Barbary Coast," he says. "It was a neighborhood filled with every vice know to man: saloons, prostitution, opium, dance halls, and taverns."[9]

Tyler says the more he read, the more he realized that this level of San Francisco history does not exist any longer. "[It was as if] it were swept out into the bay after the earthquake and re-established as the financial district it is today."[10]

Because of this, Tyler wanted Wayfare to be something that celebrated the city's past. "I wanted to bring a bit of history back to a neighborhood that seemed to have lost its identity—a restaurant for and by San Francisco."[11]

Once he made the decision to fashion Wayfare after restaurants of old, he says they went on a yearlong hunt

"Please mind your top hats, overcoats and umbrellas," it says on the home page of Wayfare Tavern's website. Tyler wanted to recreate a dining experience from the early twentieth century.

into libraries and historical societies, trying to find out what restaurants looked like in the late 1800s.

"Most of San Francisco burned in 1906," Tyler says. "So the real images were hard to find. [But we did find] a book from 1910 called *Bohemian San Francisco*, written by Clarence Edgar Edwords. It was the Holy Grail."[12]

According to Tyler, the book describes the restaurant scene in San Francisco before the earthquake "in such detail that I could smell what they were eating," he said. The author also describes the café society of the day as "Wayfarers," or people who are world travelers with their thumbs on the pulse of art and culture.[13]

"Once we had the name, the design fell into place," Tyler says. "We reimagined the space as a tavern that San Franciscans of distinction have been dining in for over a hundred years. I love [this] restaurant. It's one of my proudest achievements."[14]

Today, Tyler says he has a couple of hundred employees, whom he loves with all of his heart. He also says that his crew is really tight and that he manages them through texts and emails when he is not in town.

"I work all the time," he says. "Success is not easy and it is not free. The second you take a day off, that is the second that the wheels get shaky."[15]

In a day and an age when a majority of restaurants fail, maybe this commitment is what has sustained Wayfare—that and good food, of course. "I'm onsite a lot and always have a wide peripheral vision to see what is happening every day," Tyler adds.[16]

"The restaurant business is a game of nickels," Tyler adds. "I will often take two garbage bags and pour them out and bring my staff in to see all the dollar bills that we let go that evening. It is all about refining your strategy, being committed to superior customer service, and not being afraid to make a mistake. When you make a mistake, you've plugged a hole that you will not go into again."[17]

Through the Eyes of Critics

The atmosphere of Wayfare Tavern is classic San Francisco. "With its golden eagle emblem, black and dark colored wood accents, brushed-metal plates and cushy booths, the service is as welcoming as Tyler Florence's television persona itself," says Elaine Wu, a writer with *Bay Area Eats*. "Our server was at once knowledgeable, warm, and genuinely excited about the food coming out of the kitchen."[18]

Meanwhile, San Francisco restaurant critic Michael Bauer says, "the generous portions and the style of food mirror the feel of the interior—masculine and American—with stuffed animal heads on the walls and pewter service plates on the tables."[19]

And, the menu is exactly what you would expect from Tyler's cooking style. It's a "greatest hits compilation of sophisticated American comfort food with a slight French slant," Elaine says.[20]

The menu includes such things as deviled eggs, steak tartare, pork hash, macaroni and cheese, carrot cake, and of course, Tyler's signature California fried chicken with fried herbs.

"I'd seen Tyler Florence make fried sage on his show, *Tyler's Ultimate*, but never expected to enjoy the mellow, almost nutty flavor to pair so well with the chicken's perfectly thin, crisp crust," Elaine says. "The flavorful chicken benefitted from the buttermilk brine, creating a moist, tangy meat. I've tried a lot of fried chicken at various places around San Francisco, but this was clearly the best in my book."[21]

Meanwhile, Elaine says, the mac and cheese is smooth and creamy. "I'm not a fan of baked, clumpy, greasy versions of the dish. And the mild yet distinct garlic flavor was prevalent in the breadcrumbs, which is a good thing. I wish, though, that the cheese had more kick and depth. The jack cheese didn't give it enough flavor power like I'd hoped. Regardless, it was still a decadent pleasure."[22]

Michael, on the other hand, raves about the seared octopus, which he says is a brilliant dish "plated with a charred scallion hollandaise, cipollini onions and a slightly chunky linguica [a garlicky smoked pork sausage] puree. On a subsequent visit, I ordered the octopus again, and it was even better."[23]

As for dessert, the carrot cake and the chocolate cream pie definitely take the cake according to Elaine and Michael. For Elaine, the most impressive dessert was the carrot cake, which was not only rich and moist, but also came with a pool of carrot syrup that surrounded it. "Everyone at the table wanted to drink it straight," she says. "It tasted like spiced cider, rich with cinnamon and cloves. It was sweet, spicy, and heavenly."[24]

Meanwhile, Michael says he wants to put the chocolate cream pie in his dessert hall of fame. "I thought it was going to be too much—the crust holds a layer of devil's food cake, pudding, salted caramel ganache and whipped cream—yet it all comes together flawlessly."[25]

Michael says he was also enamored with the restaurant's huge doughnuts served with three sauces.

Overall, Elaine says the evening was capped off when she mentioned to the server that one of her dining companions was celebrating a birthday. Not only did the server bring a dessert with a candle on it, but the birthday treat also included a note signed personally by Tyler.

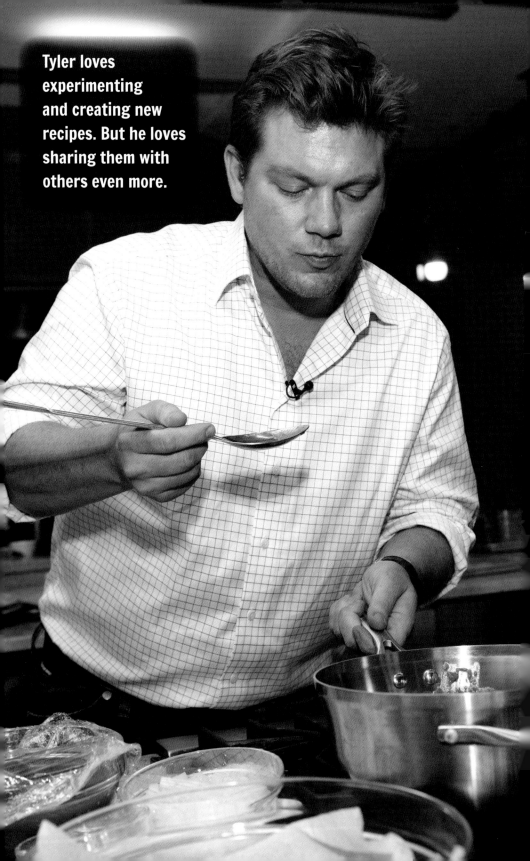

Tyler loves experimenting and creating new recipes. But he loves sharing them with others even more.

 ## Tyler Pays Homage to Other Successful Restaurants

According to the Food Network, there are several restaurants around the United States of which Tyler is particularly fond.

Kumamoto Oysters at Hog Island Oyster Co. in San Francisco

Tyler says he would eat raw oysters every day of his life. Kumamoto Oysters grows their own oysters in Tamales Bay and sells them at their San Francisco restaurant as well as distributing to other restaurants.

Bacon and Egg Pork Belly Confit at Bottega Napa Valley in Yountville, California

Chef Michael Chiarello serves pork belly that has been salted and braised in olive oil, cut into cubes, seared, and broiled with a coating of powdered sugar. Then, it is served with stewed peppers and a breaded and fried soft-boiled egg.

S'More Pie at Buckeye Roadhouse in Mill Valley, California

Chef Robert Price uses a graham cracker base, chocolate, toasted almonds, and a marshmallow meringue topping to take the campfire favorite to a whole new level.

Salumi Cone at Boccalone Salumeria in San Francisco

Chris Cosentino is steering the salumi revolution on the West Coast at Boccalone. For his salumi cone, customers choose from different meats: capocollo (KA-po-Koh-lo; a dry cured pork), guanciale (goo-an-CHI-al-ay; made from pork jowls or cheeks), lardo (lar-DOH; made from combining pork fat with herbs and spices) , prosciutto (pro-shoot-oh; a thin-sliced salty ham), pancetta (pan-CHET-tah; similar to bacon), and lonza (LONE-zah; made by cool curing and spice rubbing a pork shoulder). Salumi is more commonly called "salami" in the United States, even though salami is just one kind of salumi. A salumeria is a shop or restaurant that specializes in salami.

Pollo al Forno at Barbuto in New York

Tyler thinks Barbuto chef Jonathan Waxman's chicken is the best; even better than his own. The oven-roasted chicken is served with an Italian salsa verde made from capers, garlic, herbs, and anchovies.

Phat Burger with Bacon and Cheese at Pearl's Deluxe Burgers in San Francisco

Pearl's Deluxe Burger just happens to be located around the corner from Tyler's shop. The burgers are made from 80 percent lean ground chuck and are seared on a flat top. The Phat Bob burger is topped with bacon, lettuce, tomato, onion, and sharp cheddar. Tyler likes his burger rare, just barely seared.

Pimiento Cheese with Flatbread at Magnolia's Uptown/Down South in Charleston, South Carolina

One of Tyler's favorite foods is pimiento cheese—because it is such a Southern flavor. Pimiento cheese is often referred to as "the caviar of the south." It is a spread made from cheddar cheese, pimento peppers, cream cheese, spices, and mayonnaise. Every southern cook has his or her own take on this dish. Tyler worked for Chef Donald Barickman right out of culinary school, so he has a special appreciation for his restaurant, Magnolia's Uptown/Down South.

Roasted Chanterelle and Truffle Cheese Pizza at Serious Pie in Seattle

When you think of Seattle, you probably don't think of pizza, but Serious Pie is a serious pizza place. The crust is prepared like bread dough, and the pie is baked in an applewood-burning brick oven. Chanterelle mushrooms are slightly sweet, while while truffles have an earthy taste that compliments the cheese in a fantastic way.

Crab Roll at Fish in Sausalito, California

You can get a lobster roll anywhere on the East Coast, but according to Tyler, on the West Coast you should get a Dungeness crab roll. In Fish's crab roll there is nothing to hide the crab's succulent flavor. Fish restaurant cooks with ecologically conscious, sustainable ingredients.

Grilled Corn on a Stick at Café Habana in New York

Tyler thinks the grilled corn at Cafe Habana is delicious: traditionally grilled corn, coated in *Cotija* cheese, chili powder, and mayonnaise. It's spicy, salty, sour, and sweet.

Sand Dab Fillets at the Tadich Grill in San Francisco

At the Tadich Grill, the third-oldest restaurant in the United States, the sand dab fillets are prepared with a simple, old-school recipe. The fish is breaded lightly and pan-fried, then served with a white wine-butter sauce, vegetables, and crispy fries.

Popovers at BLT Steak in New York

A popover is a pastry that combines elements of a soufflé and a muffin. BLT Steak serves their Gruyère-topped popovers in place of bread, so it's complimentary. The recipe isn't secret though—the restaurant includes it in the basket of popovers.

BBQ Pulled Pork Sandwich at Charlie Vergo's Rendezvous in Memphis, Tennessee

Rendezvous has been around since 1948, and is an infamous Memphis eatery. The pulled pork sandwich stands out in a city known for it's barbecue. It features slow-smoked pork with a spicy and sweet barbecue sauce and coleslaw on a soft bun.

Marin Joe's Special at Marin Joe's in Madera, California

Egg, ground beef, spinach, and caramelized onions combine to create this unique and delicious dish. And Marin Joe's has great ambiance—it's considered an institution in the area.

Grilled Cheese and Tomato Soup at Muir Woods Trading Company Café in Muir Valley, California

Tyler loves to take his son to the Muir Woods Trading Company Café, located in Muir Woods National Park. The café has an amazing grilled cheese and tomato soup. The sandwich is made with local, organic, nine-grain bread, tomato, and Mt. Tam cheese. It's served with homemade organic tomato soup that's great for dunking. Tyler says it's a real hidden gem.[26]

"He wasn't even in town, let alone in the restaurant at the time of our meal," Elaine says, "but it's these personal touches in the service, the food, and décor that make this restaurant standout."[27]

Even today it is difficult to secure a reservation, Michael says. "The crowds continue to come and [Tyler's] career continues to blossom . . . [He] has proven himself up to the task of running a complex restaurant. His celebrity may bring diners in the door, but the staff and the food keep them coming back."[28]

Other Restaurants

In addition to Wayfare Tavern, Tyler also opened two other restaurants in 2010. These include Rotisserie & Wine in Napa Valley and El Paseo in Mill Valley. He also opened a spin-off of Rotisserie & Wine, known as Napa Farms Market in the San Francisco Airport. However, he has since closed Rotisserie & Wine.

Originally, Tyler closed the restaurant for a remodel during the off-season. But when it didn't quite come to fruition, he announced that he was closing it for good. "We just want to consolidate and focus our efforts on our other two restaurants, Wayfare Tavern and El Paseo," Tyler explains. His restaurant at the airport remains open as well.[29]

El Paseo

In 2010, Tyler joined forces with Sammy Hagar, the guitarist and vocalist who replaced David Lee Roth in the rock band Van Halen. Together, they took over the upscale restaurant El Paseo in Mill Valley and reopened it with a new concept.

Tyler is very hands-on at his restaurants and other business ventures. It is important that if his name is on something, it lives up to his reputation and standards.

"[At the time] it was a French restaurant with a Spanish name owned by a Japanese company," Tyler says. "It was a bit of a disconnect there."[30]

Tyler and Sammy kept the restaurant's name but turned it into an American tavern. Their idea was to serve food prepared with ingredients only from Marin County.

"Other than salt, pepper and wine, everything will [come from Marin County]," Tyler says.[31]

The atmosphere of the venue, originally built as artists' studios in the 1940s, fit perfectly with their plans. Designed by noted architect Gus Costigan, who sketched his designs while serving in World War II, "El Paseo is a soulful and authentic example of the California Mission-Style," according to the restaurant's website.

El Paseo was Tyler's third restaurant in the Bay Area, joining Rotisserie & Wine in Napa Valley and Wayfare Tavern in San Francisco.[32]

Napa Farms Market

Napa Farms Market is an artisan marketplace celebrating the best of Northern California's agricultural bounty right in the airport. According to their website, it doesn't matter what you are craving, you will be able to create a picnic to go that makes your flight more delicious. It's also a great place to pick up last-minute Bay Area food gifts for friends.

What's more, the eatery has won every major airport concession award and has been named "Best Airport Restaurant" by *Food & Wine Magazine*. Even Virgin's Sir Richard Branson considers the food spot one of his favorite airport restaurants.

Chapter

4

Tyler's
Cookbooks

Known for his uncomplicated recipes, fresh food, and interesting flavors, Tyler has traveled around the country not only learning about local cuisines, but also helping everyday people improve their cooking. As a result, he has developed a unique perspective on how American people like to eat and cook.

According to *Lifestyle Food*, Tyler "believes in the type of cooking that comes from a 'real kitchen'—a place dedicated to culinary honesty." So, it is not surprising that Tyler, a leading chef recognized by top publications like *Food & Wine*, *GQ*, the *Wall Street Journal*, and *People*, is also a best-selling author of numerous cookbooks that focus on "real kitchens" around the country.[1]

The majority of Tyler's cookbooks center around fresh ingredients and focus on what the average person would be most interested in. Whether the aspiring home cook is looking for simple food that can be prepared anytime, dinners for guests, or fresh food for kids, Tyler's cookbooks are ones that

Tyler believes in using fresh ingredients and bold flavors. His cookbooks center around easy-to-follow instructions that are meant to be used by everyday cooks.

TYLER FLORENCE FRESH

anyone could use with ease and enjoy every minute of it. All in all, Tyler has written nine cookbooks as well as three children's books: *Tyler Makes Pancakes*, *Tyler Makes Spaghetti*, and *Tyler Makes Birthday Cake*.

Tyler Florence's Real Kitchen

His debut cookbook, *Tyler Florence's Real Kitchen: An Indispensable Guide for Anybody Who Likes to Cook*, was published in 2003. In it, he shows the home cook how to prepare simple meals that taste amazing. And the list of recipes inside is as diverse as it is long. Overall, it includes simple meals that taste amazing, comfort-food classics, and even a few new dishes for those who are feeling adventurous.

According to the book's description, this cookbook stays true to Tyler's cooking philosophy. Cooks will be taught how to "use great, simple ingredients and then let the natural flavors speak for themselves."[2] Inside, recipes include things like cold fried chicken, a perfect meatloaf, and drop-dead lasagna.

This cookbook is well liked by most who purchase it. In fact, one reviewer says: "I've tried recipes from virtually every chef on the Food Network but Tyler's recipes are the only recipes that have consistently turned out good, if not great. His show *Food 911* has provided several staples in our household, which are very easy to cook and prepare. With that in mind, I decided his book would be an excellent idea to buy and quite frankly, it is. The recipes are wonderful, savory, and enjoyed by everyone— even kids."[3]

Adding to the List

In 2006, Tyler wrote his second cookbook, *Tyler's Ultimate: Brilliant Simple Food to Make Any Time*. This book is based

Debunking Common
★ Myths About Steak

Myth #1: You should always marinate a steak. According to Tyler, a wet marinade will steam the meat and it won't give you that golden brown crust. So be sure that you do not marinate your steaks the next time you are prepping them for the grill.

Myth #2: Season your steaks liberally with salt and pepper. Instead, skip the pepper when seasoning raw steak, Tyler suggests. Pepper burns at a high heat and develops a bitter flavor. However, you should always liberally season a raw steak with a good kosher salt. But hold off on the pepper until after it is cooked.

Myth #3: Grill marks make a steak look more appetizing. According to Tyler, grill marks are nothing more than burnt meat. Instead, you want the Maillard reaction, which occurs when the amino acids and carbohydrates on the surface of the steak melt when applied to high heat. It is what creates that coveted caramelized crust.

Myth #4: Always test the steak with a thermometer. Tyler says a cake tester will work just as easily. Simply poke the center of the steak, then press the tester to the bottom of your lip. "If it is above body temperature, then it is a perfect medium-rare steak," he says.

Myth #5: Make your steak fancy. Of course there is nothing wrong with preparing a steak in a fancy manner, but why not use an easier way? Tyler suggests melting the fatty steak trimmings down and using them to baste the steak after it comes out of the oven. He also recommends topping the steak with some compound butter.[4]

on his belief that every meal should be the ultimate dining experience. Throughout the cookbook, he encourages readers to make every meal a special occasion with friends and family.

In 2008, Tyler wrote the best-selling cookbooks *Stirring the Pot* and *Dinner at My Place*. And in 2010 he wrote *Tyler Florence Family Meal: Bringing People Together Never Tasted Better.* In 2011, Tyler wrote the book *Start Fresh: Your Child's Jump Start to Lifelong Healthy Eating* in an effort to inspire parents to cook fresh food for their children.

"Cooking for my children means more than just going through the motions of getting dinner on the table. It's about forging the foundation for a healthy relationship with food that will last for the rest of their lives," Florence writes in the book.[5]

Tyler says he improved his cooking-for-kids skills with his own children, first with his oldest son, Miles, and later with his son, Hayden, and daughter, Dorothy. "Everything in the book is tested on my own children."[6]

> *"Cooking for my children means more than just going through the motions of getting dinner on the table. It's about forging the foundation for a healthy relationship with food that will last for the rest of their lives."*

In 2012, Tyler tried his hand at writing children's books, creating *Tyler Makes Pancakes!* This book is about Tyler and his dog, Tofu, and their hunger for blueberry pancakes. Then, in 2013, he wrote *Tyler Makes Spaghetti!,* which again features Tyler and Tofu. And in 2014, he added *Tyler Makes Birthday Cake!* to the list of Tyler and Tofu adventures.

In his 2012 cookbook, *Tyler Florence Fresh,* Tyler shows off his bold side with a celebration of fresh everyday foods prepared in innovative and delicious ways. According to the book's description, Tyler uses each fresh ingredient as a launching pad and builds innovative dishes flavor by flavor. He also shows readers how to put easy-to-find ingredients to work in unexpected ways.

"To me, the idea of doing something very pure felt appealing this time around," Tyler says. "It's incredibly stripped down— we wanted to branch out and do something different that felt fresh."[7]

When writing a cookbook like *Fresh,* Tyler says the first thing he does is lock himself in his office and start writing flavor profiles. He makes a list, brainstorms, and then clarifies the concept. Then he tests the recipes and makes edits.

"The content has to be perfect," he says. "When I'm cooking, I can adjust things easily, but that's not necessarily true for people at home. They take the recipe as a Bible."[8]

Tyler's inspiration for the cookbook came from the country's battle to live healthy lives. "One of the biggest hurdles right now is health care. We are becoming a very unhealthy nation that's expensive to care for. Heart disease, diabetes, high blood pressure—all diet. This is a controllable thing. I just want to continue the conversation . . . I want to talk about what "fresh" really means. It's not a sell-by date, but a philosophy. It's putting fresh food in the body and treating it as a machine."[9]

One interesting aspect to the cookbook is that it is not organized by categories like main dish, side dish, and appetizers.

Tyler's love of his family inspired him to create a line of all natural baby foods, called Sprout.

★ Cooking at Home

Tyler spends a lot of time teaching other people how to cook. Whether it is his viewers on television or his cookbook readers, he is always offering tips, sharing techniques, or giving advice. But what is he like at home, when no one is watching but his family?

Who cooks more at home? "My wife, Tolan, and I split cooking duties in the house," Tyler says. "I think our children actually prefer her cooking over mine. I think I get a little too fancy with the spices sometimes. Her slam-dunk dish is her turkey meatloaf; mine is pancakes on the weekends."[10]

What does he eat when he is home alone? "If I'm home alone, which is almost never, I like to chop raw vegetables and make a giant salad," Tyler says. "We keep the vegetable crisper packed with treasures from the farmers' market."[11]

What inspires him to cook at home? "I'm . . . inspired by the amazing ingredients our farmers are pulling out of the ground every day and the ranchers we cultivate a relationship with that get us one step closer to the truth," he says. "I follow a ton of very talented chefs on Instagram, the brightest people in the business . . . but we try not to do things that other people are doing. If you get a box of heirloom tomatoes, quiet your mind and listen to the tomato—I mean, really understand it. Building a dish from it that respects the four-month-long struggle to create such a dynamic flavor can be the most inspirational moment that season."[12]

What is in the fridge that might surprise people?

"Homemade baby food—most store-bought baby foods are highly processed, and it's really easy to make healthy versions at home," he says. "And a bottle of Dom, because you never know."[13]

How would you describe working in your kitchen?

"At home with family and friends and wine and music, it's relaxed," he says. "Professionally, it's intense."[14]

What is his cooking routine like?

Tyler says they are very busy in his house, so they treat Sundays as cooking day. ". . . On Sunday we try to get ahead of everything. We spend the whole day in the kitchen. It's fun. We'll make two soups and put them in individual bags in the freezer, make cookies. We make sauce for pasta, with ground turkey as a base."[15]

A lot of chefs, like Tyler, recommend prepping ahead of time in order to make weeknight meals easier. By planning and prepping ahead of time, you can make sure you are eating healthily and making good choices.

Tyler Dishes on His Favorite (and Least Favorite)
★ Ingredients

Tyler says his pantry expands and shrinks all the time with flavors and ingredients he is experimenting with. Here are a few of his favorite ingredients. And while Tyler is a lover of all foods and flavors, there is one thing he will never put in his mouth. Check it out.

Fresh herbs: "For me there is no comparison between fresh herbs and dried—I use only fresh. They add an intense, bright flavor to foods and are widely available. With the exception of oregano, I think dried herbs taste muddy."[16]

Spanish paprika: "It's smoky and rich and tastes meaty when you bite into it."[17]

Lemon: "[It] is key—a couple drops of juice can really open up the flavor of a dish that's falling flat.[18]

Salt: "I can't live without good salt. My favorite is Sicilian sea salt, because it tastes like dehydrated seawater."[19]

Olive Oil: "I'm much more into olive oil than butter," he says.[20]
" . . . One thing I'm really into right now is smoked olive oil. It's made by a wonderful mom and pop company based in Sonoma. They have patented the ability to cold smoke olives before they're crushed. It's one of the sexiest things I've ever tasted.[21]

Soy Sauce: "And then there's soy sauce. I . . . love Asian food because the flavors are mind-blowingly complex; mix soy sauce with some ginger and chili paste—it's so delicious.[22]

Coffee: A favorite flavor? "The taste of coffee, especially really good espresso."

Miso: "But I'm also a big fan of miso. I think my last meal would be the black cod miso at Nobu. Either that or a big bowl of guacamole."[23]

Quinoa: "Quinoa is a South American grain considered to be the same value of gold during the Aztec period in Central America. It's one of those real, amazing super foods that I like a lot."[24]

Chicken: When asked what three ingredients he would choose if he was only allowed to have three. Tyler chose quinoa, olive oil, and chickens. "I'd have a chicken coop in my backyard, and when they stop producing eggs, cook the chicken."[25]

The infamous hundred-year-old egg: "During a trip to Hong Kong, I was walking through the street food stalls with the intention of eating everything I could and decided

to try the infamous hundred-year-old egg. It was preserved in lye; when it was cracked open, the yolk was black and snotty and smelled horrible. That's when I drew the line on what I would and wouldn't put in my mouth."[26]

Tyler demonstrates how to make his version of oysters Rockefeller: oysters on the half shell, topped with greens and copious amounts of butter.

Instead, the cookbook is organized by ingredients. Tyler says he did this intentionally.

"I don't use the table of contents when I cook," Tyler explains. "I use the index. We wanted to increase searchability to the recipe [that the readers] want."[27]

Inside the Test Kitchen: 120 New Recipes, Perfected

When developing this cookbook, which is designed to look like a Moleskine notebook, Tyler not only wrote the book but also did the majority of the photography work as well. The recipes in the book were developed along with his test kitchen staff and are fresh and approachable. Overall, the recipes are a selection of classic American dishes and comfort foods that Tyler has given a makeover.

Inside the Test Kitchen is designed for the home cook, who wants to put a "crowd-pleasing dinner" on the table. Meanwhile, one reviewer says the kitchen geek who wants scientific proof that the cheese she is putting in her mac and cheese has the highest possible stretch factor would also enjoy the book.[28]

When coming up with ideas for the book, Tyler reached out to his Twitter followers asking: "What do you want to learn how to cook?" and told them to respond with the hashtag #tftest-kitchen. Then, in the introduction of the book, he pointed out that his followers are not a quiet group.[29]

"You inspired me," he writes, "while asking for everything from homemade bacon pancakes to French onion soup. In truth, this book was born on social media."[30]

Tyler's much-talked-about test kitchen is above his Mill Valley restaurant, El Paseo. It is a studio apartment that has been converted into a small cooking lab. Inside this kitchen, he

This illustration from *The Opera of Bartolomeo Scappi* shows a medieval kitchen.

came up with the 120 recipes that he included in his book *Inside the Test Kitchen*.

Without television cameras to worry about or line cooks to instruct, the lab is where Tyler says he comes to think about what he has absorbed as a chef. Then, he takes that knowledge and combines it with food science to make classic recipes better.

"We're adding to the conversation by detangling recipes and making them straightforward, creating a cleaner, easier way to cook," he says.[31]

Tyler's Picks: His Favorite Cookbooks

When Tyler graduated from culinary school in the early 1990s, the first big wave of celebrity chefs included Charlie Palmer, Emeril Lagasse, Charlie Trotter, Jean-Louis Palladin and Mark Miller. Not surprisingly, he devoured their cookbooks, looking for inspiration. "Mark Miller's *Coyote Café*, all of their cookbooks, I just consumed and slept with them under my pillow hoping through osmosis I would extract more out of them."[32]

Tyler says he also loves cookbooks that are special little oddities. For instance, *The Opera of Bartolomeo Scappi*, written in 1540, is one that comes to mind.

"Scappi was arguably the world's first celebrity chef. He cooked for the Pope and wrote his book . . . with small drawings of bizarre kitchen tools, and recipes for strange things like door mice," Tyler says. "Seriously: They would keep mice in small cages and feed them figs soaked in wine, then roast them or fry them whole. It's just bizarre! But it's also beautiful. It shows you we do have a pretty antiseptic idea these days of what's edible and what's not edible."[33]

Tyler says he's also a big fan of René Redzepi's book, *Noma*. "I've seen so many culinary trends come and go, and it's nice to see something like the naturalism that's happening now, this new interest in foraged foods, where the excitement is not so much about the wizardry of cooking but the flavors of foods you'd otherwise walk right by—like wood sorrel, or Douglas fir shoots."[34]

Tyler says he likes the idea that "you could pick those in the spring and lightly steam them to give a dish this wild flavor that you might smell in a shampoo but never think about eating, I think that's marvelous." What's more, Tyler says he encourages his employees to forage. "They'll take an afternoon or morning and fill some deli containers with whatever they find, to bring in and add to a dish. I think that's so great—keep your eyes open, there's a lot more out there edible than you might think."[35]

Chapter 5

What It Means to Be a Celebrity Chef

Tyler Florence's vision of a chef is expanding every day. In addition to delighting audiences on the Food Network and cooking great food at his restaurants, he is exploring other business ventures that complement who he is as a celebrity chef.

"The business opportunities that come up all have to be taken very seriously," Tyler says. "It all has to fit comfortably inside [the] brand. For me, everything we do has to answer two questions: Is it world-class? And is it delicious."[1]

Sprouting Ideas

One business venture that Tyler is particularly excited about is his line of baby food, known as Sprout Organic Foods. The idea first came to mind when a friend was visiting his home and having trouble getting her toddler to eat.

"We were at my New York apartment when the idea for Sprout first popped up," he says. "A friend brought her toddler

Tyler is both a celebrity and a chef. He often attends food events, book signings, and television premieres, where he takes photos with fans and signs autographs.

---

over, and she had a little jar of something that was absolutely terrible. Every spoonful that went in, her son would spit out. She started crying. So I grabbed a couple of carrots, steamed them, pureed them, and fed it to him. His eyes lit up, and he started grabbing for the bowl."[2]

Before Sprout Organic Foods came along though, Tyler said he would classify baby food as more like medicine than actual food. "As a parent, there was nothing out there that I felt good about buying. It was just gruel."[3]

So he wanted to give parents an alternative. Tyler says many parents think that children have no palate or taste for adult foods. But he believes that if you give kids "something that actually tastes good, they'll appreciate you for it. And they'll start developing a palate for a plant-based diet instead of fried, salt, and carbohydrates."[4]

"Children have ten times the ability to taste as adults do, so it's important that we start getting them accustomed to good food early on in their life," Tyler says. "They'll make sure to give you clues as to what they don't like," he adds with a laugh, as he's had to accommodate his three children's developing tastes.[5]

To further help parents feed their kids healthy foods, Tyler also is helping spearhead a new app called Yumavore. People who use the app will be able to share their custom recipes and pictures all in one platform.

Dabbling in a Little Bit of Everything

Tyler has a knack for spotting a good thing. He is always willing to take risks and expand his culinary empire. Here are just a few of the things he is involved with.

Tyler Florence Wine

In 2009, Tyler began his winemaking when he partnered with Michael Mondavi of Mondavi Family Winery, a fourth generation winemaker in the southern tip of Napa Valley. Today, he works with a number of different growers to create unique flavor combinations for his wines.

"As a chef, one of the things I love best about putting together recipes is experimenting with ingredients and combining flavors with perfect balance to find the truth of flavor," he says. "It turns out this is also one of my favorite things about making wine."[6]

★ Healthy Food for Kids

Research shows that if kids are not introduced to certain foods before the age of three, their response to new things is often a fight or flight reaction. Basically, kids instinctively believe that strange-tasting things, like a weird new vegetable, might hurt them.

To make sure kids get on the right path to healthy eating, Tyler suggests creating a vegetable-based diet as soon as possible. What's more, he says that roasting, his favorite vegetable cooking technique, will help too.

"You can roast *any* vegetable and it tastes amazing," he says. "Everyone has a sheet pan, a knife, and some olive oil. Roasting helps bring out the natural sweetness and caramelization of almost any vegetable."[7]

Tyler also believes that adult food can be kids' food too and should not be separate at mealtime. "Pull kids into the decision-making process, and have a meaningful discussion about dinner," he suggests. "It can be scary for them to be surprised by what's on the table. And don't let them throw a tantrum and spoil dinner for everyone!"[8]

To do this, Tyler has what he calls "Blending Sessions", where he selects grapes by hand from Sonoma County vineyards. He then blends them together to produce wine for his customers to enjoy with great food.

According to his website, the Blending Sessions are "inspired by what happens when he closes the doors to the blending room and crafts the story of that year's harvest. Rather than being married to one particular vineyard, [Tyler] and a new brigade of other California winemakers can be mercenaries for great grapes, picking their favorite grapes from different regions and blending them into a one-of-a-kind experience."[9]

"Tyler has always been known to experiment with different ingredients to combine flavors for the perfect balance," says Chelsea Madren, a writer for the *Examiner*. "The same technique is used to make wine, selecting varietals from different areas to make the perfectly balanced wine."[10]

Overall, Tyler's winemaking has been successful. He has won twenty-nine medals and consistently scored in the 90s from wine critics.

Cricket Flour

As odd as it sounds, flour can be made from crickets and it "tastes like dark toast," Tyler says. In fact, about four thousand crickets go into one cup of Bitty Foods' cricket flour, which probably explains why the company's twenty-ounce bag costs about twenty dollars.[11]

Still, Bitty Foods founder Megan Miller sees a bright future for the products. And apparently, so does Tyler. He became an equity investor in the company after seeing Megan's TEDxManhattan Talk. In fact, Tyler says he imagines cricket flour "as a staple" in a new line of products.[12]

Tyler likes to have his hand in every aspect of a meal, including what people drink! In 2009, Tyler began making and bottling his own wine.

Megan markets her products as the future of food. Apparently, crickets reach maturity in six to eight weeks and can live on next to nothing. So she can farm fifty thousand pounds a month from a tiny warehouse. This means that the energy they are using to produce cricket flour is minimal. What's more, people who follow a Paleo diet may find the flour appealing. The Paleo diet is based on the idea of eating the way humans did during the Paleolithic era—meaning no agriculturally produced products such as wheat.[13]

There is a warning label on the flour though. It indicates that if you are allergic to shellfish, you also may be sensitive to crickets and should not consume products with cricket flour in them.[14]

Consulting for Applebee's

In 2006, Tyler partnered with Applebee's, a national chain of bar and grill restaurants. The goal was to help them improve their menu, not only making it taste better, but also making it a little bit healthier. But Tyler was relentlessly criticized in the culinary world for working with the company.

"If you are going to affect change, you have to affect change at a high level," Tyler says. "Applebee's paid me a lot of money … for ten recipes and ten days of my life. We were talking about taking them to a whole new simpler, pure direction that I think that brand really needed."[15]

During Tyler's time consulting with them, the chain added some roasted chicken options instead of fried. They also had conversations about going organic. According to Tyler, the campaign got Applebee's "pretty far" in terms of change. But in the end, he quit working with the brand "because we got such negative press about it."[16]

Creating a Drool-Worthy Kitchen

Because the kitchen is where Tyler spends the bulk of his time, it is not surprising that he worked with an interior designer to help create *House Beautiful*'s annual Kitchen of the Year in 2011. The twenty-six-hundred-square-foot structure was constructed on the outdoor plaza at Rockefeller Center in New York. Then, during its display, he and a number of other chefs manned the kitchen's multiple stoves offering cooking demonstrations.

"We [gave] it this rustic, romantic touch," Tyler says. "It's definitely a Northern-California-inspired kitchen. Ina Garten is a really talented home cook, and she designed an incredible

Only Time
★ Would Tell ...

One story that Tyler loves to share occurred when he was a fifteen-year-old living in Greenville, South Carolina. He saved the little money he made washing dishes and went to the local Kmart store and "bought the dream of teenage boys everywhere at the time, a Timex watch."[17]

"It had a gold-colored face and a fake alligator strap," Tyler says. "I think things that are more difficult to make are to be cherished for their humanity and craftsmanship. I have the same affection for chef's knives that are well engineered."[18]

But from those humble beginnings of purchasing his first watch emerged an all-consuming love for fine timepieces. Tyler's collection now includes sixteen watches. He started his collection with the Panerai Luminor, an Italian-made watch. He bought the timepiece in 1997 to celebrate signing his first network contract.

"I'm not a snob," Tyler says. "Having a power watch is about a quiet sense of strength. It makes a statement that says you're successful."[19]

Which he is.

space a couple of years ago that felt like her East Hampton home. Jeff Lewis did it last year, and it was very LA. We wanted to build something that feels like this beautiful Northern California approach, with some heft to it. It definitely has a manly feel to it."[20]

To give the kitchen its "manly feel," Tyler says he and the interior designer took a look at Edwardian service kitchens for inspiration. "We wanted a big, oversized island that would feel like you could feed an army off of it [where] everyone could gather around."[21]

"It's a gigantic service kitchen with lots of interesting bits and pieces that make it feel very specialized," Tyler adds. "For instance, there's a rolling butcher's cart that snaps into the counter, which is right in front of the two double ovens. [During the] holidays or [on] Thanksgiving, you'd take your

"At the end of the day, you can slice a mushroom in about three inches of space, and you can carve a chicken in a foot and a half. So it doesn't matter how big the kitchen is."

turkey out of the oven, put it on the butcher's block and then roll it out to the dining room. And there's a knife rack that goes along the side of it. It feels like a professional kitchen."[22]

Tyler also developed the kitchen with a large outdoor component. "For me, the Northern California experience is about being able to cook out of a wood-roasting oven, and to eat outside," Tyler explains. "So we decided to break it up into two different big kitchens—we have an amazing outdoor

House Beautiful
Kitchen of the Year
WITH
TYLER FLORENCE

WITH Tastes of Summer
ROCKEFELLER CENTER
JULY 18–22

Presented by
TISHMAN SPEYER

HOUSEBEAUTIFUL.COM/KOTY

Tyler was lucky enough to be able to create his own dream kitchen. And in 2011, *House Beautiful* magazine called his the Kitchen of the Year.

Setting Up Your
★ Kitchen at Home

According to Tyler, it really doesn't matter how big your kitchen is to cook a great meal. What really matters is how you set up your space.

"At the end of the day, you can slice a mushroom in about three inches of space, and you can carve a chicken in a foot and a half," he says. "So it doesn't matter how big the kitchen is. What matters is how well you organize three spaces [the refrigerator, the prep station, and the oven or cooking area] to form a triangle."[23]

Additionally, Tyler says the triangle you form in your kitchen does not have to be perfect. The important thing is that you have a well-organized area where you can reach for the things you need when you are cooking, like your knives or a cutting board, and they are already there.

Tyler says the essentials of any good kitchen include a solid set of pots and pans, three knives [a chef's knife, a paring knife, and a bread knife] and a good-size cutting board. "You want to be able to cut two chickens or chop enough vegetables for dinner, and actually get some work done," he explains.[24]

But he says not to worry too much about the size of your kitchen. "You can make the same meal in any size kitchen."[25]

entertainment space and kitchen, as well as inside. It just gives people options when they look at how they want to build a house. Instead of having your guests outside when someone's stuck in the kitchen cooking, let's just take the kitchen outside as well."[26]

No Need to Shop Around

Although currently closed, perhaps one of the most interesting ventures Tyler has taken on is the Tyler Florence Shop in Mill Valley, California. According to the Food Network, cooks of every level delighted in all the chef-inspired goods found there. Walls of artisan cookware, expertly crafted jams, chocolates, spreads; even a cozy cookbook library, where guests can relax and gather some cooking inspiration.

"Everything else I've done my entire life was defined by the Food Network," Tyler says. "The retail store was the first time I showed what I was thinking."[27]

And people loved it. For instance, Farmhouse Urban blogger Serena Armstrong said, "The Tyler Florence Shop is so jam-packed with goodies for the home, and in particular the kitchen, it is truly a feast for the eyes. Not only that, but the store is laid out almost like a living space—a magazine worthy living space filled with beautiful things that will surely enhance your culinary talents."[28]

According to Armstrong, Tolan Florence was actually the talent behind the incredible selection of merchandise that includes serving pieces, stemware, copper cookware, and just about every cooking and baking gadget a person could imagine. There was also a selection of vintage and antique items, like saltboxes and herb planters.

The Tyler Florence Shop in Mill Vally, California sold cookware, kitchen appliances, and specialty ingredients. Tyler also often gave culinary demonstrations and had hopes of attaching a full-service restaurant.

"Tolan searched flea markets and estate sales, and picked up things on her travels to create these charming collections.[29]

Visitors also found Tyler's own label of salts and spices, Dean & Deluca dried herbs, Barefoot Contessa baking mixes, and Stonewall Kitchen beverage mixers among the offerings. And at the far end of the store was a "drop-dead gorgeous kitchen where Tyler occasionally cooks for private events."[30]

"The kitchen was angled from the corner—not a typical kitchen layout, but one that works well for such purposes," Serena added in her review. "Standing in the space, I also find it extremely efficient. The sink and cooktop are almost directly

Tyler's line of marinades, sauces, and spice blends was quite popular.

opposite one another, while the other appliances and storage is all within a few steps."[31]

Susan Dyer Reynolds, a writer for *Northside San Francisco*, agreed that the shop was a sight to behold. "Tyler Florence's retail store is more drool-worthy than the best-stocked Williams-Sonoma, and features everything from French copper cookware to antique chopping blocks to Marin County preserves."[32]

It truly is a reflection of Tyler's personality and his passion for cooking. And Tyler agrees. "I love what I do—I love doing live demos and getting people excited about food and cooking. I am jazzed to be me for a living."[33]

In 2012, Tyler wanted to expand the demonstration kitchen in order to have more space for classes. As construction began, they came across difficulties and had to close. Due to zoning and lease problems, the store was still closed as of 2016. However, Tyler, Tolan, and their team are fighting a legal battle to have it reopen as soon as possible.

Chapter

6

Tyler's Causes

Most celebrity chefs, like Tyler, do more than appear on television, run restaurants, write cookbooks, and sign endorsement deals for cookware. In fact, many of them are working to change the country's food system. Some are also helping to educate the public about the importance of healthy eating, even on a budget.

For instance, Tyler has long been involved in the fight against hunger and has worked with the San Francisco-Marin Food Bank, the New York City Food Bank, and other similar organizations. He also is passionate about teaching people to eat healthy foods.

The "Drink Good Do Good" campaign in 2015 teamed Tyler up with Naked Juice, nonprofit organization Wholesome Wave, and other celebrities like Adrien Grenier (of HBO's *Entourage*). The goal was to help bring fresh fruits and vegetables to areas and neighborhoods where fresh fruits and vegetables are hard to find. They were hugely successful, donating the equivalent of five hundred thousand pounds of fresh produce.[1]

According to the event producers, nearly twenty-four million Americans live in food deserts (meaning they do not have access to affordable, quality, fresh fruits and vegetables). Meanwhile, Naked Juice, a division of PepsiCo, packs a bounty of fruits and vegetables into every bottle of its juices and smoothies and believes everyone should be able to enjoy these foods every day. So a partnership with Wholesome Wave, an organization that helps create affordable access to fresh, local and regional food to those in need, seemed like a natural fit.[2]

Throughout the campaign, Naked Juice donated ten pounds of produce to Wholesome Wave any time someone took a selfie with fresh fruits and vegetables and tagged it with #DrinkGoodDoGood.

"It means that anybody with a banana or something can make a contribution—which is huge," Tyler says. "It doesn't take a lot to get fresh food and produce [to people in under-served communities]—it takes money and effort and desire."[3]

Understanding Food Insecurity

Being hungry is a feeling that more people in the United States experience than you might realize. In fact, one in seven US households struggles to afford food. This is referred to as food insecurity. Yet despite the number of food-insecure families in the country, many in need do not take advantage of safety net programs available to them such as WIC, SNAP, and free school meals.

Health advocates are trying to change this fact by encouraging qualified families to access breakfast at school. For instance, ten million kids who qualify for free lunch at school do not eat breakfast there. There are several reasons why this might happen. First, breakfast is often served before classes

Tyler uses social media to bring attention to his causes.

start, and it is hard for parents to get their kids to school early. Another possible reason is that children often feel too ashamed to admit to their classmates that they qualify for a free meal.[4]

"If we want to be successful economically, if we want to reduce health care costs, and if we want to ensure our national security, then we also have to see child nutrition in the way we see so many issues involving national security and economic security and health care security," says Tom Vilsack, agriculture secretary. "It's a critically important part."[5]

Tyler says the question is: "How do big corporations get involved in getting more nutrients into these dark corners of our cities. I really applaud [Naked Juice] for jumping into this because it's a mission I [have cared] about for twenty years."[6]

How Many People Lived in Food-Insecure Households?

In 2014:

48.1 million people lived in food-insecure households.

12.4 million adults lived in households with very low food security.

7.9 million children lived in food-insecure households in which children, along with adults, were food insecure.

914,000 children (1.2 percent of the nation's children) lived in households in which one or more child experienced very low food security.[7]

As an added bonus, in last year's Farm Bill, the U.S. Department of Agriculture (USDA) and the National Institute of Food and Agriculture (NIA) allocated up to $31.5 million in grant funding for the Food Insecurity Nutrition Incentive (FINI) program. This money is available with an equal dollar match from nonfederal funds—so a large donation from a corporation like Naked Juice can actually go a long way in helping people in underserved neighborhoods gain access to fresh fruits and vegetables.[8]

Naked Juice also supports other Wholesome Wave programs, such as its Double Value Coupon Program (DVCP), which helps low-income shoppers double their spending power at more than five hundred participating farmers' markets. Through DVCP, underserved communities are provided with fresh fruits and vegetables by allowing shoppers to double the value of federal nutrition benefits from Supplemental Nutrition Assistance Program or SNAP (formerly known as food stamps) as well as their Women, Infant, and Children (WIC) funding when used at participating farmers' markets.

Meanwhile, another program that Naked Juice supports is the Fruit and Vegetable Prescription program, which helps health care providers give families innovative prescriptions that can be spent on fruits and vegetables at grocery stores, farmers markets, and other healthy food retailers. Most health care providers find the program extremely beneficial.

For instance, one health-care provider says: "The biggest thing I've seen is the FVRx program, [which] gives patients the ability to take a risk and to make change. In talking with parents, what I realized was that they wanted to come to the farmers market but didn't have the money. Now they have a reason to go."[9]

There is a sense of urgency surrounding food insecurity among chefs like Tyler. For instance, he says: "If we don't do something about [it], I don't know who will, to be perfectly honest with you . . . At the top of the business model it's just business as usual. [Restaurants and food companies] want to keep you excited and distracted and hungry, and then on a consumer level people don't know what to do. They're just concerned with [feeding] the family every night."[10]

Traveling the Country Helping the Food Insecure

Tyler also participates in events around the country to raise money for food banks and address food insecurity issues. One event that he participated in was *An Evening with Tyler Florence* as part of the Biscuit Festival in Tennessee. The festival was sponsored by the Food Network, which donated ten dollars of every ticket sold to Food for Kids.

> *"Food is the source of such great joy and creativity in the restaurant world, but there's a whole segment of the population that doesn't know where their next meal is coming from."*

Food for Kids is a joint effort between Second Harvest Food Bank of East Tennessee and the schools within their eighteen-county service area. The goal is to provide healthy meals to children in East Tennessee who may be going without regular meals. The event potentially generated $15,000, which translated into more than forty-five thousand meal deliveries to nearly six hundred kids in the area.[11]

Tyler also participated in the San Francisco-Marin Food Banks Hunger Challenge. During the challenge he had to live off of Food Bank groceries and a $4.50-per-day food budget. The Hunger Challenge is designed to simulate what it means for the more than thirty thousand households that rely on food bank groceries from the San Francisco-Marin Food Bank to supplement their SNAP benefits. When he signed on, he became the latest in a string of chefs and high-profile folks such as Mario Batali and Newark, New Jersey Mayor Cory Booker to go a week or more on food stamps.[12]

"Food is the source of such great joy and creativity in the restaurant world, but there's a whole segment of the population in San Francisco and Marin that doesn't know where their next meal is coming from," Tyler says. "I wanted to challenge myself to experience that world so I can better understand what my neighbors go through every day and to spread the word about the Food Bank."[13]

Central Kitchen executive chef cuisine Ryan Pollnow and Mina Group corporate pastry chef Lincoln Carson also signed on to the challenge. Everyone was invited to participate in the challenge. They simply downloaded a grocery list mimicking the food available at the Food Pantry every week. Those groceries were in addition to the $4.50-per-day budget they could spend on food.[14]

Cooking Healthy on a Budget

Many Americans find it hard to eat healthily, especially on a budget. In fact, according to a recent food and health survey, 52 percent of Americans believe it is easier to do their taxes than it is to figure out how to eat healthfully! What's more, when you have a tight budget for food, it sometimes seems easier to just buy junk food or processed food in order to stretch how far a dollar or two goes.[15]

But Tyler believes that cooking healthily does not have to "pinch your pocketbook." One suggestion he offers is to plan meals that share ingredients. For instance, buy ground turkey in bulk because the price per pound is cheaper and then plan several different meals using the meat.

How to Make a
Great Salad

#1 Pick freshest produce

"Buy tomatoes on the vine," Tyler says. "The vine gives tomatoes extra moisture and nutrients to provide maximum flavor long after they've been picked."

#2 Be careful with marinades

"Try to use marinades with a little oil in them," Tyler says. "The heart-healthy fats can help you absorb vitamins A and E, found in leafy greens."

#3 Use your grill

"Grill your lemons," Tyler suggests. "It may sound odd, but grilling lemons takes away the sourness and adds a slightly sweeter flavor that's tasty sprinkled over greens."

#4 Walk on the wild side

"Get a low-calorie crouton flavor by pulsing bread crumbs, garlic, parsley, olive oil, and salt and pepper in a food processor several times until crumbs turn bright green," Tyler says. "Spread the crumbs on a baking sheet, then bake until crispy [about 7 minutes]. They create a savory topping for any salad."[16]

Between his restaurants, products, cookbooks, and television shows, Tyler Florence is one of the best-known chefs in the United States.

"I think turkey is the super protein," he says. "When we're talking about making delicious food that's healthy, you really have to figure out where to cut fat but not necessarily cut flavor."[17]

Tyler says another way to cut your grocery bill is the "recession buster sitting on your kitchen shelf—a slow cooker. The great thing about a slow cooker [is that] you can make a delicious meal with inexpensive cuts of meat like pork shoulder or beef shoulder, and you can make beef stew."[18]

He also encourages people to get cooking. Not only is it cheaper than eating out, but "being a chef means that you get to operate what I call the heartbeat of the house—and that's the kitchen."[19] Lots of great memories can be made if the family works together to save money and serve creative, inexpensive and healthy meals.

From a humble beginning in South Carolina as a dishwasher, to one of the most recognized chefs in the United States, Tyler Florence has come a long way. And it's clear there's only more to come from the Food Network star. As food becomes more and more important to the average American, chefs with a conscience and a desire to educate, such as Tyler, will only gain more popularity. Fans can be certain there will be more shows, more appearances, more cookbooks, more restaurants, and other projects in the future for Tyler Florence. And if he has his way, there will be more and more chefs in the future.

"It's really important that the kids share the experience of cooking . . . It creates memories. A lot of people have sort of lost the idea of cooking. I like to bring it back where it's a big part of the family experience."[20]

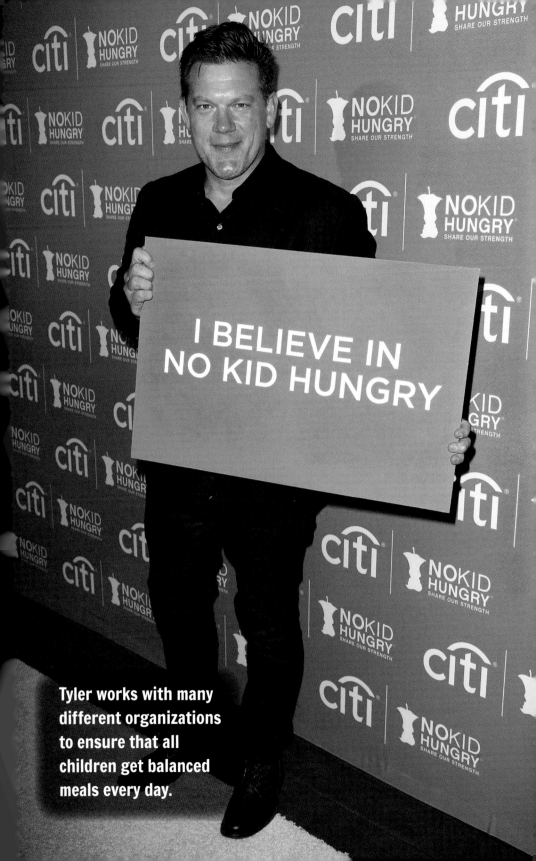

Tyler works with many different organizations to ensure that all children get balanced meals every day.

Try It
Yourself!

Corn Chowder

Serves: 8

Ingredients

2 tablespoons (30 grams) butter

2 tablespoons olive oil

1 onion, diced

2 cloves garlic, minced

1 stalk celery, diced

1 large carrot, diced

6 sprigs fresh thyme

1/4 cup (30 grams) flour

6 cups (1.5 quart) vegetable stock

4 medium-size Yukon Gold potatoes, scrubbed and diced

2 cups (475 mL) heavy cream

(1) 12-ounce (350 milliliters) can of corn, or 6 ears of corn, roasted and cut from cob

Salt and pepper, to taste

Chives or parsley for garnish

Directions

1.) Heat butter and 1 tablespoon of olive oil in a large soup pot. Add the onion, garlic, celery, carrots, and thyme and cook until the vegetables are fragrant. Season with salt and pepper.

2.) Sprinkle the flour over the vegetables, stirring to coat. Cook for about 1–2 minutes.

3.) Add vegetable stock and bring to a boil.

4.) Add potatoes and let the soup boil heavily for about 8 minutes, or until the potatoes begin to soften.

5.) Add the cream and the corn kernels.

6.) Simmer for about 10–12 minutes, or until the potatoes are fully cooked and the corn has fully flavored the broth.

7.) Drizzle with additional olive oil and ladle into soup bowls. Serve with crusty bread, if desired.

Fettuccine Diavola

Serves: 4

Ingredients

1 pound (450 grams) fettuccine

2 12 ounce (350 milliliters) cans crushed tomatoes

1/4 cup (40 grams) roughly chopped, pitted black olives

1 onion, chopped

3 cloves garlic, minced

1 teaspoon crushed red pepper

¼ cup (60 milliliters) olive oil

Fresh basil

2 bay leaves

Directions

1.) Heat olive oil in a large skillet. Add garlic and sauté on medium-high heat until it starts to become fragrant. Add crushed red pepper.

2.) Add the chopped onion and olives, reducing heat to medium-low.

3.) Gently tear apart the basil and add it to the oil, vegetables, and spices.

4.) Once the onions are translucent, add the crushed tomatoes, juice and all. Add bay leaves. Stir until all ingredients are combined. Reduce heat to low and allow to cook until sauce begins to thicken (about 12 minutes).

5.) Meanwhile, in a large pasta pot, bring water to a boil. Generously salt with sea salt. Add the fettuccine, fanning around the pot so the pasta doesn't stick together while it cooks. Cook for about 7–8 minutes, or until al dente.

6.) Drain the pasta and add it to the large skillet with your sauce. Using tongs, gently fold sauce and pasta together. You can serve this family style (on one large dish), or plate it individually. Garnish with ricotta salata and basil, and more crushed red peppers if you'd like an extra kick!

Spicy Black-Eyed Peas

Serves 6–8

Ingredients

2 slices thick-cut bacon, diced

4 cloves of garlic

4 dried chiles

2 bay leaves

1 pound (450 grams) dried black-eyed peas

4 cups (1 quart) chicken stock

2 tomatoes, diced

Salt and pepper, to taste

1 lemon, juiced

Olive oil (as needed)

Fresh thyme

Directions

1.) In a large pot, cook the bacon until crispy. Remove bacon and set aside.

2.) Add the garlic to the hot bacon fat. Gently crush the dried chilies between your palms and place in the grease. (Be sure and wash your hands before you touch your face!)

3.) Add the bay leaves and the dried peas.

4.) Stir in chicken stock and the tomatoes.

5.) Simmer for about an hour, or until the peas are soft.

6.) Add the fresh thyme, pulled from the stem, lemon juice, bacon pieces, and a drizzle of olive oil. Add salt and pepper, if desired. Serve as a side with pork chops or fried chicken, or over rice for a vegetarian meal.

Baked Mac and Cheese

Serves 6–8

Ingredients

1 pound (450 grams) elbow macaroni

5 tablespoons (75 grams) butter

4 cups (1 quart) whole milk

4 cloves garlic

1/2 medium onion

1 clove

1 bay leaf

3 sprigs of fresh thyme

2 tablespoons (30 milliliters) flour

2 cups (180 grams) grated sharp cheddar cheese

1 cup (90 grams) chunked cheddar cheese

1/2 cup (45 grams) grated Parmesan cheese

1 cup (90 grams) Monterey jack cheese

Salt and pepper to taste

Directions

1.) In a large pan, melt one tablespoon of butter, until it coats the bottom of the pan.

2.) Add the milk, clove, onion, garlic, bay leaf, and thyme to the melted butter and bring to a boil. Once boiling, remove from heat and set aside.

3.) In a separate pan, melt the remaining butter and add flour, stirring until a thick paste forms, about 3–4 minutes. Do not let the roux brown.

4.) Strain the vegetables and herbs from the milk and slowly whisk the milk into the roux. Season with salt and pepper.

5.) Whisk constantly to avoid lumps until the sauce begins to thicken, about 5 minutes. Remove from heat.

6.) Stir in the grated cheddar and Monterey jack cheeses, until the cheese is melted and fully incorporated in the sauce.

7.) In a separate pot, bring water to a boil. Add the macaroni until just shy of al dente, or a few minutes short of the package's recommended cooking time. Drain pasta.

8.) Spray a large casserole dish with cooking spray. Pour in the pasta and top with the sauce. Stir pasta and cheese sauce together, until all the noodles are coated in sauce. Level with spoon.

9.) Top with chunked cheddar and parmesan cheeses.

10.) Bake at 350°F (176° C) until the top is golden and bubbly, about 25 minutes.

Ultimate Beef Stew

Serves 4–6

Ingredients

1/4 cup (60 milliliters) olive oil

3 tablespoons (45 grams) butter

1 cup (120 grams) flour

3 pounds (1,350 grams) beef chuck shoulder
roast cut into 2-inch pieces

1 tablespoon (20 grams) paprika

6 cups (1 ½ quarts) beef broth

A handful of fresh thyme sprigs

3 fresh rosemary sprigs

3 bay leaves

6 cloves of garlic, diced

2 bay leaves

4 large carrots, sliced

2 stalks celery, sliced

2 cups (300 grams) pearl onions

2 cups (300 grams) porcini or portobello
mushrooms, diced

6 large Yukon Gold or red skin potatoes,
scrubbed, peeled, and diced.

Salt and pepper, to taste

Directions

1.) In a large soup pot, heat olive oil.

2.) On a large platter, season the beef with salt, pepper, and paprika. Add the flour and coat the meat.

3.) Place the beef in one layer in the hot oil, browning on each side. Be sure not to overcrowd the pan. You might have to work in batches. Each piece of meat should have a golden crust on each side. Set the beef aside when it's browned.

4.) Add the stock to the hot pan, using a wooden spoon to scrape up all the tasty seasonings and flour that are at the bottom. Bring to a simmer.

5.) Add the browned meat, celery, onions, carrots, potatoes, garlic, rosemary, bay leaves, and thyme. Season with a bit more salt and pepper.

6.) Bring to a boil, then reduce heat. Simmer until all the juices start to thicken. Cover and slowly cook for about 2 hours, or until the vegetables are cooked and the beef is tender.

7.) Add mushrooms and a drizzle of olive oil. Bring heat up to low, allowing the broth to boil.

8.) Cook for an additional 7–8 minutes, or until the mushrooms are soft. Remove the rosemary, thyme sprigs, and bay leaves before serving.

Sautéed Shrimp

Serves 2

Ingredients

1 pound (450 grams) jumbo shrimp, peeled and deveined

1 teaspoon paprika

2 tablespoons (30 milliliters) olive oil

2 garlic cloves, minced

2 shallots, minced

1 lemon, juiced

Salt and pepper, to taste

Fresh chopped parsley for garnish

Directions

1.) In a large saucepan, heat olive oil over medium heat.

2.) Add shallots and garlic.

3.) Add the shrimp, salt, pepper, and paprika.

4.) Stir until all the shrimp are coated in spices, vegetables, and oil. They will cook very quickly, so reduce heat to low.

5.) Keep everything on one layer, and turn the shrimp over after two minutes. Cook another minute, and remove from heat.

6.) Toss the shrimp in olive oil and garnish with parsley.

All-American Meatloaf

Serves: 6

Ingredients

1½ pounds (680 grams) ground beef

1 pound (450 grams) ground pork, lamb, or turkey

1 cup (150 grams) unseasoned breadcrumbs

3 eggs

1 large onion, diced

4 cloves garlic, diced

3 stalks of celery, diced

1 teaspoon paprika

3-4 sprigs of thyme, leaves removed

½ teaspoon ground cayenne

Salt and pepper, to taste

(1) 6-ounce (180 milliliters) can tomato sauce

Directions

1.) Prepare a large loaf pan by spraying it with cooking spray.

2.) Preheat oven to 350° F (176° C).

3.) In a large bowl, combine ground meats, breadcrumbs, eggs, onion, garlic, celery, thyme, cayenne, salt, and pepper. Using your hands, knead ingredients until well mixed.

4.) Place meat mixture into loaf pan, pressing into the corners and sides. Top with paprika.

5.) Bake for about an hour, or until the meat is brown and sizzling. Top with tomato sauce and bake for an additional 15 minutes, or until the meat is cooked all the way through.

6.) Serve by slicing like you would a loaf of bread; vegetables and mashed potatoes make a classic combination.

Ultimate Fried Chicken

Serves 4–6

Ingredients

4–6 pounds (1814-2722 grams) of chicken, cut
  into pieces (thighs, wings, legs, breasts)

4 cups (1 quart) buttermilk

2 eggs

Whole head of garlic, roasted and smashed

2 tablespoons dry, rubbed sage

2/3 cup (160 milliliters) olive oil

3 cups (360 grams) flour

2 tablespoons garlic powder

2 tablespoons onion powder

2 tablespoons paprika

2 tablespoons cayenne pepper

Salt, pepper to taste

2 tablespoons hot chili sauce

A handful fresh sage

A handful fresh thyme

3 large sprigs of rosemary

Lemon wedges

Peanut or canola oil, for frying

Directions

1.) In a gallon-size Ziploc bag, combine the pieces of chicken with the olive oil, sage, roasted garlic pepper, and a generous amount of salt. Add about 1/3 cup of water, or just enough that the chicken is fully submerged. Refrigerate at least 2 hours (or up to overnight).

2.) In a large, shallow platter (or bowl) combine flour and spices (be sure to use plenty of salt and pepper) until well blended (you can use a sifter if you'd like, or simply use a spoon or your hands).

3.) In another large bowl, whisk together the buttermilk and egg with the hot sauce.

4.) Drain the chicken and pat it dry.

5.) Fill a large frying pan (cast iron or a Dutch oven is best) about halfway with oil. Place over med-high heat. Add the sage, thyme and rosemary. This will flavor the oil while it heats (you can also add the garlic from your marinade).

6.) Dip the chicken pieces individually in the buttermilk mixture, then dredge in the flour and spice mixture liberally.

7.) When the oil has reached 350–365° F (176–185°C), gently place the pieces of chicken in the hot oil. Do not overcrowd the pan. You'll most likely have to work in batches. If you don't have a candy thermometer to check the oil's temperature, you can throw a sprinkle of flour into the oil. If it sizzles heavily right away, your oil is hot enough.

8.) Make sure the chicken turns golden brown on each side (you may have to turn each piece with a long pair of metal tongs after about 6 minutes). Remove chicken and herbs when it's finished (about 12 minutes), using a wire skimmer or a pair of metal tongs.

9.) Place chicken on a large platter that has been covered with newspaper or paper bag and a paper towel. This will absorb extra oil. Sprinkle the chicken with salt and pepper while the oil is still warm.

10.) Repeat steps 7–9 until all the chicken is cooked. Crush the fried herbs and garlic, and sprinkle over the chicken. Serve with a wedge of lemon.

Ultimate Lemon Blueberry Cheesecake

Serves: 6

Ingredients

Crust:

- 2 cups (240 grams) graham cracker crumbs, finely ground
- 1 stick butter, melted
- 1/2 teaspoon cinnamon

Filling:

- 2 8 ounce packages (450 grams) of cream cheese, softened
- 3 eggs
- 1 cup (200 grams) granulated white sugar

1 pint (450 mL) sour cream

Zest of one lemon

1 teaspoon vanilla extract

Topping:

1 pint (450 mL) blueberries

2 tablespoons sugar

1 lemon, juiced and zested

Directions

1.) Using a light cooking spray, grease a springform pan.

2.) Combine the graham cracker crumbs, melted butter, and cinnamon in a mixing bowl. Stir with a fork until the crumbs are fully coated in the butter. This will still have a crumbly (not doughy) consistency, but should be easy to mold.

3.) Pour the crumb mixture into the springform pan.

4.) Using a measuring cup or a smooth glass, gently press the crumbs into the pan, allowing the mixture to form along sides, creating a well for the cheesecake batter.

5.) Once crust is smooth, refrigerate for at least 5 minutes.

6.) In a large mixing bowl, beat the cream cheese. Start with the lowest setting on your electric mixer, then gradually increase the speed until the cream cheese is light and fluffy. Reduce speed back to low.

7.) Add the eggs, one at a time, until mixture is smooth, creamy, and buttery in color.

8.) Add the sugar and sour cream slowly, beating until well combined.

9.) Add the lemon zest and vanilla. Be sure and use a rubber spatula around the sides of the bowl (once the mixer is off!), to make sure that all ingredients are combined and that there are no lumps in the batter.

10.) Pour the filling into the crust in the springform pan, smoothing over the top with your spatula. The filling may come over the crust. This is absolutely fine.

11.) Create a water bath for your cheesecake, using a large baking pan with high sides. Hot water should come up about halfway up the springform pan. Wrap the springform pan in aluminum foil, so that no water may leak into your crust, causing it to be mushy.

12.) Bake cheesecake in water bath for 40–45 minutes at 350° F (176° C). It will still be soft and slightly wiggly in the middle when you take it out. Refrigerate 4–5 hours.

13.) In the meantime, using a small saucepan, combine blueberries, lemon juice and zest, and sugar. Bring to a boil.

14.) Very quickly, you will see the blueberries bursting and a sauce beginning to form. It will only take about 5 minutes for the sauce to be thick, gooey, and fragrant.

15.) Once the cheesecake has hardened, remove it from the springform pan. Cut into slices and serve with the warm blueberry sauce on top.

Banana Nut Bread

Serves: 6

Ingredients

2 cups (420 grams) all-purpose flour

1 1/2 teaspoons baking powder

1/2 teaspoon salt

4 overripe bananas

1 cup (120 grams) granulated white or raw sugar

3/4 cups (1 1/2 sticks) butter, melted (but cooled)

2 large eggs

1 teaspoon cinnamon

1 teaspoon vanilla

1/2 cup (75 grams) chopped nuts such as pecans or walnuts

Directions

1.) Butter and flour a loaf pan. Preheat oven to 350° (176° C).

2.) In a large mixing bowl, combine flour, baking powder, and a pinch of salt.

3.) Mash two of the bananas with a fork, so they still have some texture.

4.) In a mixer, whisk the remaining two bananas with the sugar, to create a fluffy banana whip.

5.) Add the butter, eggs, vanilla, and cinnamon to the whipped bananas, mixing until well combined. Be sure and use a rubber spatula to get everything off the sides of the bowl.

6.) Add the flour mixture slowly, stirring after each addition. Make sure everything is incorporated, but do not overmix the batter.

7.) Fold in the mashed bananas and nuts.

8.) Pour the batter into prepared pan. Give the pan a nice slap on the counter a couple of times to remove any air bubbles.

9.) Bake for about 1 hour and 15 minutes, or until the bread is golden brown, and when a toothpick is inserted into the center, it comes out clean. It will most likely crack down the middle, but that's absolutely fine. It will just give the bread a little extra crunch and texture.

10.) After bread cools, use a knife to separate the bread from the sides of the pan. This will make it practically fall out of the pan.

11.) Slice and serve with a little extra butter, if desired.

Books

Tyler Florence's Real Kitchen: An Indispensable Guide for Anybody Who Likes to Cook (March 25, 2003)

Tyler's Ultimate: Brilliant Simple Food to Make Anytime (April 12, 2005)

Dinner at My Place (October 1, 2008)

Stirring The Pot (October 2008)

Tyler Florence Family Meal: Bringing People Together Never Tasted Better (October 12, 2010)

Start Fresh: Your Child's Jump Start to Lifelong Healthy Eating (June 7, 2011)

Tyler Florence Fresh (December 4, 2012)

Eat This Book: Cooking with Global Fresh Flavors (December 4, 2012)

Tyler Makes Pancakes! (Tyler and Tofu) April 24, 2012

Tyler Makes Spaghetti! (Tyler and Tofu) April 23, 2013

Tyler Makes a Birthday Cake! (Tyler and Tofu) April 22, 2014

Inside the Test Kitchen: 120 New Recipes, Perfected (October 28, 2014)

Restaurants

Wayfare Tavern

El Paseo

Napa Farms Market

1971—Born in Greenville, South Carolina

1986—Began working in a restaurant in Greenville, South Carolina at fifteen years old

1992—Relocated to New York City after graduating from Johnson & Wales

1996—Made his television debut in 1996 with guest appearances on Food Network

1998—Ventured out on his own, becoming the executive chef at Cibo before opening critically acclaimed Cafeteria in Manhattan's trendy Chelsea neighborhood

1999—Took over *Food 911* on the Food Network

2003—*People* magazine named Tyler the "sexiest chef alive" Also wrote his first cookbook, *Tyler Florence's Real Kitchen*

2004—Married Tolan Clark

2006—Moved to California when Tolan became pregnant with their first child; provided consulting services to Applebee's to improve their menu

2008—Opened his first retail shop in Mill Valley, California

2009—Began making his own wine

2010—Opened Wayfare Tavern in San Francisco's financial district as well as El Paseo restaurant with rocker Sammy Hagar in Mill Valley

2011—Created *House Beautiful's* Kitchen of the Year

2014—Wrote his twelfth book, *Inside the Test Kitchen*

Chapter 1:   The Beginnings of a Chef

1. "Q&A with Chef Tyler Florence," *Taste*, Williams-Sonoma, March 19, 2013, http://blog.williams-sonoma.com/qa-with-chef-tyler-florence (Accessed October 2015).
2. Ibid.
3. "Tyler Florence Biography," *Biography.com*, http://www.biography.com/people/tyler-florence-20928957#renowned-chef%2Ftv-personality (Accessed October 2015).
4. Cole, Jennifer V., "Fast Talk: Tyler Florence," *Travel and Leisure*, June 22, 2009, http://www.travelandleisure.com/articles/fast-talk-tyler-florence (Accessed October 2015).
5. Reynolds, Susan Dyer, "10 Questions with Tyler Florence," *Northside San Francisco*, http://northsidesf.com/dec08/coverstory_tylerflorence.html (Accessed October 2015).
6. Cole, Jennifer V., "Fast Talk: Tyler Florence."
7. "Q&A with Chef Tyler Florence."
8. Reynolds, Susan Dyer, "10 Questions with Tyler Florence."
9. "About Charline Palmer," Charlie Palmer Group, http://www.charliepalmer.com/about/ (Accessed October 2015).
10. "The Project," The Marta Pulini's Restaurant, http://www.martabibendum.it/en/ (Accessed October 2015).
11. "Tyler Florence Celebrity Chef," *Lifestyle Food*, http://www.lifestylefood.com.au/chefs/tylerflorence/ (Accessed October 2015).
12. "Tyler Florence Biography."
13. Hirsch, J. M., "Tyler Florence Opens Up About His Failures (And Successes)," *Huffington Post*, December 7, 2012, http://www.huffingtonpost.com/2012/12/07/tyler-florence_n_2258624.html (Accessed October 2105).
14. "Q&A with Chef Tyler Florence."
15. Ibid.
16. Reynolds, Susan Dyer, "10 Questions with Tyler Florence."
17. Morell, Katie, "Tyler Florence: Shaking Up the San Francisco Dining Scene," American Express, https://www.americanexpress

.com/us/small-business/openforum/articles/building-an-empire-tyler-florence/ (Accessed October 2015).

18. "Tyler Florence," Food & Wine, http://www.foodandwine.com /contributors/tyler-florence(Accessed October 2015).

19. Ibid.

20. Ibid.

21. Ibid.

22. Ibid.

23. Ibid.

24. Cole, Jennifer V. ,"Fast Talk: Tyler Florence."

25. Bennett, Sarah, "Q&A With Tyler Florence, Host of the Food Network's *Great Food Truck Race*," *Side Dish*, November 30, 2012. http://sidedish.dmagazine.com/2012/11/30/tyler-florence / (Accessed October 2015).

26. Ibid.

27. Ibid.

28. Andrews, Avital, "Chef Tyler Florence Carves Out His Niche," *Sierra Magazine*, July/August 2015. http://www.sierraclub.org /sierra/2015-4-july-august/artifact/chef-tyler-florence-carves-out-his-niche(Accessed October 2015).

29. Ibid.

30. Ibid.

31. "Q&A with Chef Tyler Florence."

Chapter 2: The Making of a Star

1. Hirsch, J. M.,"Tyler Florence Opens Up About His Failures (And Successes)" *Huffington Post*, December 7, 2012. http://www .huffingtonpost.com/2012/12/07/tyler-florence_n_2258624.html (Accessed October 2015).

2. Barmann, Jay, "Tyler Florence Knows Not All Food Network Chefs Are Created Equal," *Grub Street*, February 26, 2013. http:// www.grubstreet.com/2013/02/tyler-florence-celebrity-sf-food-network-chefs.html(Accessed October 2015).

3. Ibid.

4. "Q&A with Chef Tyler Florence," *Taste*, Williams-Sonoma, March 19, 2013. http://blog.williams-sonoma.com/qa-with-chef-tyler-florence(Accessed October 2015).

5. Ibid.

6. "How to Boil Water," Food Network, http://www.foodnetwork.com /shows/how-to-boil-water.html?oc=linkback (Accessed October 2015).

7. Barmann, Jay, "Tyler Florence Cooked for President Obama, Eddie Vedder at Tampa Fundraiser," *Grub Street*, September 21, 2012 http://sanfrancisco.grubstreet.com/2012/09/tyler-florence-obama-fundraiser-vedder.html# (Accessed October 2015).

8. *Great Food Truck Race*," Food Network, http://sanfrancisco .grubstreet.com/2012/09/tyler-florence-obama-fundraiser-vedder.html# (Accessed October 2015).

9. "Changing the Landscape of the Culinary Industry: Host Tyler Florence on Season 6 of *The Great Food Truck Race*," Food Network Blog, August 19, 2015. http://blog.foodnetwork.com /fn-dish/2015/08/tyler-florence-on-season-6-of-the-great-food-truck-race/?oc=linkback (Accessed October 2015).

10. Ibid.

11. Ibid.

12. Ibid.

13. Ibid.

14. Ibid.

15. Myers, Dan, "Tyler Florence's Advice for Aspiring Food Truck Owners," *The Daily Meal*, September 4, 2015, http://www .thedailymeal.com/eat/tyler-florence-s-advice-aspiring-food-truck-owners (Accessed October 2015).

16. Ibid.

17. Ibid.

18. "Changing the Landscape of the Culinary Industry."

19. Myers, Dan, "Tyler Florence's Advice for Aspiring Food Truck Owners."

20. Ibid.

21. "Food Court Wars," Food Network, http://www.foodnetwork.com /shows/food-court-wars.html?oc=linkback (Accessed October 2015).

22. "Worst Cooks in America: Top 10 Cooking Mistakes," Food Network, http://www.foodnetwork.com/shows/worst-cooks-in-america/photos/worst-cooks-in-america-top-10-cooking-mistakes.html?oc=linkback (Accessed October 2015).
23. Ibid.
24. Ibid.
25. Ibid.
26. "Top 5 Kitchen Mistakes to Avoid," Care2.com, February 1, 2013, http://www.care2.com/greenliving/top-5-kitchen-mistakes-to-avoid.html#ixzz3w0gm7O60 (Accessed October 2015).
27. "America's Best Cook," Food Network, http://www.foodnetwork.com/shows/americas-best-cook.html?oc=linkback (Accessed October 2015).
28. Hirsch.
29. Ibid.
30. Ibid.
31. Ibid.
32. Ibid.

Chapter 3:   Tyler and His Restaurants

1. "Q&A with Chef Tyler Florence," *Taste*, Williams-Sonoma, March 19, 2013, http://blog.williams-sonoma.com/qa-with-chef-tyler-florence (Accessed October 2015).
2. Hirsch, J. M., "Tyler Florence Opens Up About His Failures (And Successes)" *Huffington Post*, December 7, 2012.
3. "Q&A with Chef Tyler Florence."
4. Morell, Katie, "Tyler Florence: Shaking Up the San Francisco Dining Scene," American Express, https://www.americanexpress.com/us/small-business/openforum/articles/building-an-empire-tyler-florence/ (Accessed October 2015).
5. Ibid.
6. Ibid.
7. "Q&A with Chef Tyler Florence."
8. Ibid.
9. Ibid.

10. Ibid.
11. Ibid.
12. Ibid.
13. Ibid.
14. Ibid.
15. Morell, Katie, "Tyler Florence: Shaking Up the San Francisco Dining Scene."
16. Ibid.
17. Ibid.
18. Wu, Elaine, "Is Tyler Florence's Wayfare Tavern Worth the Hype?" *Bay Area Eats*, June 19, 2011, http://ww2.kqed.org /bayareabites/2011/06/19/is-tyler-florences-wayfare-tavern-worth-the-hype/ (Accessed October 2015).
19. Bauer, Michael, "Tyler Florence's Matured Wayfare Tavern Nails Its Niche," SFGate, February 20, 2014 http://www.sfgate.com /restaurants/article/Tyler-Florence-s-matured-Wayfare-Tavern-nails-its-5249607.php (Accessed October 2015).
20. Wu.
21. Ibid.
22. Ibid.
23. Bauer.
24. Wu.
25. Bauer.
26. Food Network.com, "Tyler Florence's Best Restaurant Eats," http://www.foodnetwork.com/shows/the-great-food-truck-race /photos/tyler-florences-best-restaurant-eats.html?oc=linkback (Accessed October, 2015).
27. Wu.
28. Bauer.
29. Lucchesi, Paolo, "Napa's Rotisserie & Wine Closes," SFGate, June 7, 2012, http://www.sfgate.com/food/insidescoop/article/ Napa-s-Rotisserie-Wine-closes-Ubuntu-in-limbo-3617926.php (Accessed October 2015).
30. Finz, Stacy, "Tyler Florence, Hagar Take Over El Paseo Space," SFGate, October 8, 2009, http://www.sfgate.com/restaurants

/article/Tyler-Florence-Hagar-take-over-El-Paseo-space-3215689.php (Accessed October 2015).

31. Ibid.

32. Ibid.

Chapter 4: Tyler's Cookbooks

1. "Tyler Florence Celebrity Chef," *Lifestyle Food*, http://www .lifestylefood.com.au/chefs/tylerflorence/ (Accessed October 2015).

2. Amazon.com, *Tyler Florence's Real Kitchen: An Indispensable Guide for Anybody Who Likes to Cook*, (Clarkson, Potter: 2003). http:// www.amazon.com/Tyler-Florences-Real-Kitchen-Indispensable /dp/0609609971/ref=sr_1_6?s=books&ie=UTF8&qid=1451795587 &sr=1-6&keywords=tyler+florence (Accessed October 2015).

3. Ibid.

4. Roberts, Anna Monette, "Tyler Florence Clears Up These Steak Myths," Popsugar, June 21, 2103, http://www.popsugar.com/food /Tyler-Florence-Steak-30847040 (Accessed October 2015).

5. Florence, Tyler, *Start Fresh: Your Child's Jump Start to Lifelong Healthy Eating* (New York: Rodale Books, June 2011).

6. Ibid.

7. Bennett, Sarah, "Q&A With Tyler Florence, Host of the Food Network's *Great Food Truck Race*," *Side Dish*, November 30, 2012. http://sidedish.dmagazine.com/2012/11/30/tyler-florence / (Accessed October 2015).

8. Ibid.

9. Ibid.

10. "Q&A with Chef Tyler Florence," *Taste*, Williams-Sonoma, March 19, 2013,http://blog.williams-sonoma.com/qa-with-chef-tyler-florence (Accessed October 2015).

11. Ibid.

12. Ibid.

13. Reynolds, Susan Dyer, "10 Questions with Tyler Florence," *Northside San Francisco*, http://northsidesf.com/dec08 /coverstory_tylerflorence.html (Accessed October 2015).

14. Ibid.

15. Huget, Jennifer LaRue, "Chef Tyler Florence, a Food Network Star, Discusses Healthful Meals for Kids," *The Washington Post*, May 31, 2011. https://www.washingtonpost.com/lifestyle/home-garden /chef-tyler-florence-a-food-network-star-discusses-healthful-meals-for-kids/2011/05/26/AGYpeRFH_story.html (Accessed October 2015).

16. Florence, Tyler, *Tyler Florence's Real Kitchen: An Indispensable Guide for Anybody Who Likes to Cook*, (New York: Clarkson Potter, March 2003).

17. Cole, Jennifer V., "Fast Talk: Tyler Florence," *Travel and Leisure*, June 22, 2009, http://www.travelandleisure.com/articles/fast-talk-tyler-florence (Accessed October 2015).

18. Ibid.

19. Ibid.

20. Ibid.

21. "Q&A with Chef Tyler Florence."

22. Cole, Jennifer V., "Fast Talk: Tyler Florence."

23. Ibid.

24. Bennett, Sarah, "Q&A With Tyler Florence, Host of the Food Network's *Great Food Truck Race*."

25. Ibid.

26. Cole, Jennifer V., "Fast Talk: Tyler Florence."

27. Bennett, Sarah, "Q&A With Tyler Florence, Host of the Food Network's *Great Food Truck Race*," *Side Dish*, November 30, 2012. http://sidedish.dmagazine.com/2012/11/30/tyler-florence / (Accessed October 2015).

28. Bainbridge, Julia, "Cookbook of the Week: Tyler Florence's 'Inside the Test Kitchen," Yahoo! Food, November 12, 2014, https://www .yahoo.com/food/cookbook-of-the-week-tyler-florences-inside-the-test-102376629616.html (Accessed October 2015).

29. Ibid.

30. Ibid.

31. Kauffman, Jonathan, "Tyler Florence's Turkey Hack," SFGate, November 15, 2015, http://www.sfgate.com/recipes/article/Tyler-

Florence-s-Turkey-Hack-5893320.php (Accessed December 2015).

32. "Tyler Florence," Food & Wine, http://www.foodandwine.com /contributors/tyler-florence (Accessed October 2015).

33. Ibid.

34. Ibid.

35. Ibid.

Chapter 5: What it Means to Be a Celebrity Chef

1. "Q&A with Chef Tyler Florence," *Taste*, Williams-Sonoma, March 19, 2013, <http://blog.williams-sonoma.com/qa-with-chef-tyler-florence>(October 2015).

2. Andrews, Avital, "Chef Tyler Florence Carves Out His Niche," *Sierra Magazine*, July/August 2015, < http://www.sierraclub.org /sierra/2015-4-july-august/artifact/chef-tyler-florence-carves-out-his-niche>(October 2105).

3. Ibid.

4. Ibid.

5. Bunce, Brooke, "Tyler Florence On Picky Kids, Real Food, and Why Hot Dogs Can Sometimes Do the Trick," *Parents*, http:// www.parents.com/blogs/food-scoop/2015/08/19/diet /tyler-florence-on-picky-kids-real-food-and-why-hot-dogs-can-sometimes-do-the-trick/ (Accessed October 2015).

6. "About Tyler Florence Wine," Tyler Florence Wine, http://www .tylerflorencewine.com/about (Accessed October 2015).

7. Bunce, Brooke, "Tyler Florence On Picky Kids, Real Food, and Why Hot Dogs Can Sometimes Do the Trick," *Parents*, http:// www.parents.com/blogs/food-scoop/2015/08/19/diet /tyler-florence-on-picky-kids-real-food-and-why-hot-dogs-can-sometimes-do-the-trick/ (Accessed October 2015).

8. Ibid.

9. "Blending Sessions," Tyler Florence Wine, http://www. tylerflorencewine.com/blending-sessions (October 2015).

10. Madren, Chelsea, "Tyler Florence balances flavors in wine and cooking," *Examiner*, July 1, 2013. http://www.examiner.com

/review/tyler-florence-balances-flavors-wine-and-cooking (Accessed October 2015).

11. Rainey, Clint, "Flour Made of Crickets Exists, and It's Incredibly Expensive," *Grub Street*, August 4, 2014, http://www.grubstreet .com/2014/08/cricket-flour-bitty-foods.html (Accessed October 2015).

12. Ibid.

13. Ibid.

14. Ibid.

15. McKeever, Amy, "Tyler Florence Defends $3 Million Applebee's Partnership," *Eater*, November 14, 2012, http://www .eater.com/2012/11/14/6522339/tyler-florence-defends-3-million-applebees-partnership (Accessed October 2015).

16. Ibid.

17. Walker, Michael, "Tyler Florence Does It on Deadline," Hollywood Reporter, November 20, 2012, http://www.hollywoodreporter .com/news/food-network-chef-tyler-florence-391897 (Accessed October 2015).

18. Ibid.

19. Ibid.

20. McKeough, Tim, "Tyler Florence on His Kitchen of the Year," *New York Times*, July 13, 2011, http://www.nytimes.com/2011 /07/14/garden/tyler-florence-on-kitchen-design-qa.html?_r=1 (Accessed October 2015).

21. Ibid.

22. Ibid.

23. Ibid.

24. Ibid.

25. Ibid.

26. Ibid.

27. Hirsch, J. M., "Tyler Florence Opens Up About His Failures (And Successes)" *Huffington Post*, December 7, 2012.

28. Armstrong, Serena, "Shopping Heaven—the Tyler Florence Shop in Mill Valley," FarmHouse Urban, February 18, 2010, http://www

.farmhouseurban.com/2010/02/shopping-heaven-the-tyler-florence-shop-in-mill-valley.html (Accessed October 2015)

29. Ibid.
30. Ibid.
31. Ibid.
32. Reynolds, Susan Dyer, "10 Questions with Tyler Florence," *Northside San Francisco*, http://northsidesf.com/dec08/coverstory_tylerflorence.html (Accessed October 2015).
33. Ibid.

Chapter 6: Tyler's Causes

1. Roth, Anna, "Chef Tyler Florence Aims to Bring Fresh Produce to the Masses with #DrinkGoodDoGood," *Civil Eats*, October 13, 2015, http://civileats.com/2015/10/13/chef-tyler-florence-aims-to-bring-fresh-produce-to-the-masses-with-drinkgooddogood-2/ (Accessed October 2015).
2. "Naked Juice Launches #DrinkGoodDoGood Social Media Campaign to Generate 500,000-Pound Donation of Fruits and Vegetables to Wholesome Wave," PR Newswire, August 18, 2015, http://www.prnewswire.com/news-releases/naked-juice-launches-drinkgooddogood-social-media-campaign-to-generate-500000-pound-donation-of-fruits-and-vegetables-to-wholesome-wave-300129684.html (Accessed October 2015).
3. Roth, Anna, "Chef Tyler Florence Aims to Bring Fresh Produce to the Masses with #DrinkGoodDoGood."
4. Goldberg, Eleanor, "1 In 7 U.S. Households Struggled To Afford Food Last Year: Report," *Huffington Post*, September 10, 2015,) http://www.huffingtonpost.com/entry/1-in-7-us-households-struggled-to-afford-food-last-year-report_55f0aa03e4b093be51bd7c22 (Accessed December 2015).
5. Ibid.
6. "Food Insecurity in the U.S.," United States Department of Agriculture, http://www.ers.usda.gov/topics/food-nutrition-assistance/food-security-in-the-us/key-statistics-graphics.aspx (Accessed October 2015).

7. Ibid.
8. Ibid.
9. "Fruit and Vegetable Prescription Program," Wholesome Wave, http://www.wholesomewave.org/our-initiatives/fruit-and-vegetable-prescription-program/ (Accessed October 2015).
10. Roth, Anna, "Chef Tyler Florence Aims to Bring Fresh Produce to the Masses with #DrinkGoodDoGood."
11. "Tyler Florence event will help fight hunger in East TN," WBIR .com, May 6, 2014, http://legacy.wbir.com/story/entertainment /people/2014/05/06/tyler-florence-food-network-biscuit-festival-cooking/8779725/ (Accessed October 2015).
12. Tyler Florence Signs on to S.F. Food Bank's New Hunger Challenge," *San Francisco Weekly*, August 27, 2013,http://www .sfweekly.com/foodie/2013/08/27/tyler-florence-signs-on-to-sf-food-banks-new-hunger-challenge (Accessed October 2015).
13. Ibid.
14. Ibid.
15. Avena Ph.D., Nicole, "The American Diet," Psychology Today, August 19, 2013, https://www.psychologytoday.com/blog/food-junkie/201308/the-american-diet (Accessed October 2015).
16. "Tyler Florence's 4 Tips for Making a Super Summer Salad," *Health*, http://www.health.com/health/gallery/0,,20366688,00 .html (Accessed October 2015).
17. "Cook Healthy for Less," Oprah, March 11, 2009,http:// www .oprah.com/food/Tyler-Florences-Healthy-and-Cheap-Meals #ixzz3vxBKBEXu (Accessed October 2015).
18. Ibid.
19. Ibid.
20. Ibid.

baguettes—A long, thin loaf of French bread.

bolognese sauce (BOH-lo-nay-say)—A meat-based tomato sauce originating in Bologna, Italy.

braising—A combination-cooking method that uses both moist and dry heats: typically, the food is first seared at a high temperature, then finished in a covered pot at a lower temperature in some type of liquid.

brine—A solution of salt, water, and seasonings used to soak meat before cooking.

burrata (BOO-rat-tah)—A fresh Italian cheese made from buffalo milk, a sort of mozzarella that hasn't been fully stretched.

capocollo (KAP-oh-co-lo)—A traditional Italian pork salumi (deli meat).

caramelization—The browning of sugar used to create a sweet flavor and brown color.

cipollini onions (chip-o-lee-nee)—A smaller, flat, pale onion with flesh that is a slight yellowish color and thin and papery skins.

confit (kon-FEE)—A type of food preparation which helps the food to be preserved; in the classic French style, it means something cooked in its own fat (such as duck or goose).

Cryovac—A cooking technique that uses airtight plastic bags combined with long cook times.

culinary—Of or related to cooking.

dice—To cut something into small cubes.

food insecurity—When people lack sustainable physical or economic access to enough food.

ganache (gah-NAsh)—A glaze or filling for pastries made from chocolate, sugar, and cream.

gruel—A thin porridge made from grain with very little flavor.

guanciale (goo-an-CHA-le)—An Italian cured meat or salami made from pork cheeks.

hollandaise—An emulsion of egg yolk, butter, and lemon. It is light yellow and creamy.

knead—To manually manipulate dough until it is soft.

lardo—A type of salumi made by curing strips of fatback with herbs and spices.

linguica (lin-gwee-KA)—A form of smoke-cured pork sausage.

lonza —An Italian cured pork loin.

Michelin Guide—A series of annual guidebooks published by the French company Michelin.

palate—A person's sense of taste.

Paleo diet—A diet based on the idea of eating the way humans did during the Paleolithic era.

pancetta (PAN-chet-ah)—Italian bacon.

pavlova—Meringue-based dessert named after the Russian ballerina Anna Pavlova.

porcini (por-CHEE-nee)—Large, originally wild Italian mushrooms that are brown in color and earthy in flavor.

quinoa (KEEN-wah)— A South American grain similar to cous cous, but containing more protein, vitamins, and healthy minerals.

roasting—A type of cooking that often starts at a higher temperature to create a "crust" on the outside of what is being roasted.

salumi (sa-LOO-me)—Italian cold cuts.

tartare—A dish made with finely chopped or minced raw beef or fish and a variety of seasonings.

wayfarers —People who travel the world with their thumbs on the pulse of art and culture.

FURTHER READING

Books

The Cookbook for Teens. Mendocino, CA: Mendocino Press, 2014.

Locricchio, Matthew. *Teen Cuisine*. Seattle, WA: Skyscape, 2014.

Marchive, Laurane. *The Green Teen Cookbook*. San Francisco, CA: Zest Books, 2014.

Salkin, Allen. *From Scratch: Inside the Food Network*. New York, NY: G.P. Putnam's Sons, 2013.

Websites

Food Network
www.foodnetwork.com
> Official site of the Food Network.

Tyler Florence
www.tylerflorence.com
> Official website of Tyler Florence.

Wayfare tavern
www.wayfaretavern.com
> Official site of Wayfare Tavern in San Francisco, CA.

El Paseo
www.elpaseomillvalley.com
> Official site of El Paseo restaurant in Mill County, CA.

Napa Farms Market
www.napafarmsmarket.com
> Official site of Napa Farms Market in the San Francisco
> International Aritport.

INDEX

A

Allen, Ted, 33
Applebee's, 79
Aureole, 9

B

Barbary Coast, 43
Barbuto, 50
Barickman, Donald, 51
Best Cook in America (TV), 32
Biscuit Festival, 94
Bitty Foods, 77
"Blending Sessions," 77-78
BLT Steak, 52
Blue Ridge Mountains, 14, 17
Boccalone Salumeria, 50
Booker, Cory, 95
Bottega Napa Valley, 49
Branson, Richard, 55
Buckeye Roadhouse, 49
Burrell, Anne, 33

C

Cafe Habana, 51
Cafeteria, 10, 20
Carson, Lincoln, 95
Central Kitchen, 95
charities, 88-95
Charleston, South Carolina, 8, 50
Charlie Vergo's Rendezvous, 52
Chiarello, Michael, 49
Cibo, 10
Clark Tolan (wife), 12, 15, 28, 39, 63, 84, 87
cookbooks, 13, 15, 17, 19, 57, 59-63, 65-67, 69, 71-72. *See also* specific titles
Coppola, Francis Ford, 12
Cora, Cat, 33-34
Cosentino, Chris, 50
Costingan, Gus, 55
cricket flour, 77-78

D

DeBartolo, Lisa, 28
Dinner at My Place (book), 61
DiSpirito, Rocco, 12
Double Value Coupon Program (DVCP), 93
"Drink Good Do Good," 89-90

E

El Paseo, 38, 53, 55, 69
Essence of Emeril (TV), 24
Evening with Tyler Florence, An, 94

F

Fish, 51
Florence, Tyler
    awards, 38, 55
    baby food, 13, 37, 65, 73-74
    birth, 7
    charities, 89-95
    childhood, 7-8, 80
    children, 12, 17, 61, 63, 75
    consultant, 79
    cookbooks, 13, 15, 17, 19, 57, 59-63, 65-67, 69, 71-72. *See* specific titles
    cooking mistakes, 33-34
    cooking style, 13-14, 16-17, 46, 55
    cooking tips, 15, 63, 98
    critics and, 38, 46-47, 77
    culinary school, 8-9, 51, 71
    entertaining tips, 15-16
    food for children, 73-77, 89-95
    guest on TV shows, 10, 20, 22
    healthy cooking, 61-62, 65, 75-76, 89, 94-96, 98
    kitchen essentials, 79, 81, 83, 98
    love of outdoors, 14, 15, 17, 81, 84
    marriage, 12
    recipes, 13, 16, 24, 26, 51, 57, 59, 62, 69, 71, 75, 100-124

restaurant owner, 38-39, 41, 43, 45-47, 49-53, 55, 69, 73, 89, 98
watch collection, 80
wine, 39, 71, 75, 77
Food & Wine Magazine, 55, 57
Food Court Wars (TV), 32-33
Food for Kids, 94
"food insecurity," 90-94
Food Insecurity Nutrition (FINI) program, 92
Food Network, 10, 16-17, 20, 22, 24, 26, 29, 32-35, 39, 49, 59, 73, 84, 94, 98
Food 911 (TV), 10, 20, 22, 24, 26, 59
food trucks, 26, 29, 31-32
Fruit and Vegetable Prescription (FVRx) program, 93

G
Garten, Ina, 79, 81
Great Food Truck Face, The (TV), 10, 12, 26, 31, 37
Grenier, Adrien, 89
Guarnaschelli, Alex, 33-34

H
Hagar, Sammy, 53, 55
Hog Island Oyster Co., 49
home cooking, 22, 33, 35, 57, 59, 63, 65, 69, 73, 83
Hourigan, Jack, 24
House Beautiful's Kitchen of the Year, 79, 81, 84
How to Boil Water (TV), 10, 20, 22, 24
hunger, in the United States, 89-95

I
ingredients, use of, 24, 34, 38, 55, 57, 59, 62, 63, 66-67, 69, 75, 77, 95
Inside the Test Kitchen (book), 69-70

J
Jake's Steakhouse, 10

Johnson and Wales University, 8-9

L
Laakkonen, Rick, 10
Lagasse, Emeril, 24, 71

M
Mad 61, 10
Magnolia's Uptown/Downtown South, 50-51
Maillard reaction, 60
Marin Joe's, 52
marinades, 60, 96
Mill Valley, California, 38-39, 49, 53, 69, 84
Miller, Mark, 71
Miller, Megan, 77-78
Mina Group, 95
Mondavi, Michael, 75, 77
Mondavi Family Winery, 75, 77
Muir Woods Training Company Cafe, 52

N
Naked Juice, 89-93
Napa Farms Market, 38, 53, 55
National Institute of Food and Agriculture (NIA), 92
New York City Food Bank, 89
Noma, 71-72

O
Obama, Barack, 28
Opera of Bartolomeo Scappi, The (1540), 71

P
Palladin, Jean-Louis, 71
Palmer, Charlie, 9-10, 71
Paris (France), 8
Pearl's Deluxe Burgers, 50
Pollnow, Ryan, 95
Price, Robert, 49
Progressive American cuisine, 10

Puck, Wolfgang, 12
Pulini, Martin, 10

R

recipes, 13, 16, 24, 26, 51, 57, 59, 62, 69, 71, 75, 79, 100-124
   all-American meatloaf, 114-115
   baked mac and cheese, 107-108
   banana nut bread, 101-102
   corn chowder, 101-102
   fettuccine diavola, 103-104
   sautéed shrimp, 112-113
   spicy black-eyed peas, 105-106
   ultimate beef stew, 109-111
   ultimate fried chicken, 116-118
   ultimate lemon blueberry cheesecake, 119-120
Redzepi, René, 71-72
Rockefeller Center, 79
Roth, David Lee, 53
Rotisserie & Wine, 53, 55
Rubicon, 41, 43

S

San Francisco, 15, 28-29, 38-39, 41, 43, 45-46, 49-51, 53, 55, 89, 94-95
San Francisco International Airport, 38, 53
San Francisco-Marin Food Bank, 89, 94
Seacrest, Ryan, 12
Second Harvest Food Bank of East Tennessee, 94
Serious Pie, 51
South Carolina, 7-8, 14, 50, 80, 98
Sprout Organic Foods, 73-75
Start Fresh: Your Child's Jump Start to Lifelong Health Eating (book), 61
steak, myths about, 60
Stirring the Pot (book), 61
Sumuro, Victor, 8-9

Supplemental Nutrition Assistance Program (SNAP), 90, 93-94
Symon, Michael, 33-34

T

Tadich Grill, 51
Trotter, Charlie, 71
Tyler Florence Family Meal: Bringing People Together Never Tasted Better (book), 61
Tyler Florence Fresh (book), 62
Tyler Florence Shop, 84, 86-87
Tyler Florence's Real Kitchen: An Indispensable Guide for Anybody Who Likes to Cook (book), 59
Tyler Makes a Birthday Cake! (book), 59
Tyler Makes Pancakes! (book), 59
Tyler Makes Spaghetti! (book), 59, 61
Tyler's Ultimate (TV), 10, 20, 22, 26, 46
Tyler's Ultimate: Brilliant Simple Food to Make Any Time (book), 59

U

US Department of Agriculture (USDA), 92

V

Van Halen, 53
Vedder, Eddie, 28
Vilsack, Tom, 91

W

Waxman, Jonathan, 50
Wayfare Tavern, 16, 28, 38-39, 41, 43, 45-46, 53, 55
Wholesome Wave, 89-90, 93
Women, Infant, and Children (WIC), 90, 93
Worst Cooks in America (TV), 32-33